ROGER WILLIAMS AND PURITAN RADICALISM IN THE ENGLISH SEPARATIST TRADITION

Hugh Spurgin

Studies in American Religion
Volume 34

The Edwin Mellen Press
Lewiston/Queenston/Lampeter

Library of Congress Cataloging-in-Publication Data

This volume has been registered with The Library of Congress.

CIP

This is volume 34 in the continuing series
Studies in American Religion
Volume 34 ISBN 0-88946-678-5
SAR Series ISBN 0-88946-992-X

A CIP catalog record for this book
is available from the British Library.

© Copyright 1989 The Edwin Mellen Press.

The Edwin Mellen Press   The Edwin Mellen Press
Box 450   Box 67
Lewiston, NY   Queenston, Ontario
USA 14092   CANADA L0S 1L0

The Edwin Mellen Press, Ltd.
Lampeter, Dyfed, Wales,
UNITED KINGDOM SA48 7DY

Printed in the United States of America

for Nora

CONTENTS

INTRODUCTION

Occasionally, a charismatic religious leader appears on the world scene who is a troubler of the consciences of, many in the standing order. This troubler of the public conscience is a visionary who incenses the leaders of the existing order by insisting on revolutionary change in a corrupt, confused, or merely unenlightened society. Frequently, he is able to gain impetus, through the strength of conviction, to swing the pendulum of history into a new era. Although he is likely to be remembered as a shaper of new thought and social reform, usually the troubler of officialdom by contemporaries as a nuisance unwilling to compromise ideals and incapable of harmonizing with others. The troubler speaks out with a loud, grating voice that shakes the status quo to its very core--exposing skeletons of injustice, corruption, and complacency. Seldom is he a rational social planner, nor does he seem to be endowed with common sense. Rather, often he embraces wholeheartedly, even fanatically, a single ideal and lives for that one purpose alone. By pursuing his objectives with single-minded intensity, the troubler of the conscience is able to break through the barriers of convention accepted as axiomatic by the mass of humanity; in so doing, he pays the price of being misunderstood and persecuted.

For the seventeenth century Roger Williams (c.1603-1683),[1] the notorious maverick of the American religious scene, was a conscientious troubler who during the 1630s and 1640s disturbed the minds and souls of most major leaders in England and New England. Indeed, Williams--the well-known apostle of religious liberty and founder of the colony of Rhode Island--recognized his problematic role as a troubler of the consciences of others, calling himself one of the sons of peace who "have borne and still must beare the blurs of troublers of Israel [i.e., of the chosen people of God], and turners of the World upside downe."[1] Williams felt compelled by truth to extend the idea of religious separatsm (separation from the Church of England) to its logical conclusion of separation of church and state. Religious separatism was a notion steeped in a shaky and unpopular English religious tradition known as English separatism. Its corollary; separation of church and state, was a radical spiritual notion that threatened the very foundation of seventeenth century, Anglo-American society, yet Williams pursued with holy zeal both that ideal and the corollary notion of church-state separation.

The English separatist movement reached its peak within a decade after Williams migrated to America in 1631, having emerged publicly in England nearly fifty years before at the time of Queen Elizabeth I. During the 1640s the striking and resolute Williams, who was banished in October 1635 from the colony of Massachusetts Bay, sought to carry the separatist tradition to its logical limits by transforming the concept of separation of true believers from one specific national church into the more extensive and profound principle of an absolute separation of all churches from government interference.

The beliefs of the enigmatic, "divinely mad" Williams--as evidenced by his anonymously-published The Bloudy Tenent, of Persecution, for cause of Conscience (1644)--are a study in the power of ideas. In light of the many myths that have arisen concerning his life and thought, critical reexamination of his view is in order. The time frame of the present inquiry ranges from 1581 to 1652. In 1581 Robert Browne (c.1550-1633), a Cambridge-educated minister, formed the first separatist congregation in England, an act of open rebellion; in 1652 Roger Williams published his penultimate treatise, The Bloody Tenent Yet More Bloody. As well as an examination of Williams's doctrine, this book discusses the history of the advancement of the principles of liberty and separation as espoused by several puritan dissidents--including Browne, the first English separatists; John Smyth (c.1570-1612), the first English baptist; and John Canne (d.1667), a contemporary of Williams who became a Fifth Monarchist. The primary concern is the similitude of Williams's views to those of his predecessors.

For a variety of reasons, the case of the controversial and prophetic Williams is instructive. First, as a prominent person during America's formative years, Williams was an intellectually-significant, puritan minister. Secondly, his views are relatable to the tenets of the first English separatists. In fact, he was separatism's most famous, outspoken, and revolutionary advocate. Thirdly, Williams was a pioneer whose ideas and experiences were readily applicable to a freer society. Fourthly, the path by which Williams moved from intolerance to tolerance is intriguing as an example of the evolution and application of moral and theological principles. Williams eventually became a passionate apostle of soul liberty, yet at the time of his arrival in Massachusetts in the winter of 1631 Williams was an inflexible separatist.[2] Fifthly, separatism's most articulate spokesman, Williams was both a man of the cloth and of the world. Throughout his adult life Williams was consumed by questions regarding both civil and ecclesiastical government.

By advocating unmitigated separation of church and state, Roger Williams made a major contribution to the newly-emerging American culture. Although a few contemporaries opposed publicly all civil compulsion in matters of religion, Williams probably was the first to plead, on the basis of Scripture, for clear, complete separation and consequently for toleration of all forms of religious dissent. Williams was at the fountainhead of the maturation of liberty in the modern world. He was an incipient, yet intolerant, proto-democrat whose ideas played a major role in the progression toward religious and civil freedom for all religious dissenters. In that sense, he had a significant impact on the development of the principles of political as well as religious democracy.

In October 1635 the rulers of Massachusetts Bay banished Williams for having "broached & dyvulged dyvers newe and dangerous opinions [i.e., subversive, separatist notions], against the aucthoritie of magistrates."[3] This book is a reappraisal of those "dangerous opinions" subscribed to Williams and by other early modern nonconformists. As such, it is an attempt to fill a gap in Anglo-American intellectual history.

The extent to which Williams's novel system of thought was a revolutionary reformulation of early separatist doctrine is examined by analyzing five areas: Williams's life and thought; the separatist religious tradition as represented by the beliefs and teachings of several significant precursors and contemporaries of Williams in England and America; the similarities and differences between the nonconformist tenets of Williams and other prominent sectarians; the evolution of separatist religious thought during the late sixteenth and early seventeenth centuries, specifically how puritan radicalism was transformed by Williams and his contemporaries while crossing the Atlantic Ocean; and the relationship between church doctrine and political philosophy in the belief system of Williams and others.[4]

I believe that Williams was influenced by the theology and practice of the original English separatists and that, as a separatist of the separatists, he formulated a sweeping reinterpretation of separatist thought. To comprehend Williams's ideological roots, his separatist religious heritage must be understood. In this work Williams's theology and political philosophy is compared with the doctrinal positions of several provocative forerunners and contemporaries to demonstrate that his "newe and dangerous opinions"--so threatening to the leaders in Massachusetts--were a full application of principles of religious nonconformity developed several decades earlier by the first English separatists.[5]

This book is designed to show that Williams's thought was rooted deeply in the English separatist tradition (a view less obvious than it seems); that separatist religious thought was transformed in the New World into a radical, new theory of tolerance; that there is a significant relationship between ecclesiology and political theory in separatist thought; and that Williams and the separatists contributed greatly to the moral, intellectual, and social development of colonial New England.

The first contention is that the theological beliefs of such early nonconformists as Robert Browne, Henry Barrowe, and John Smyth provided the spiritual and ideological foundation for Roger Williams's theology, faith, politics, and polemics. A major source for Williams's belief system lies within the separatist religious tradition. The degree to which Williams expounded on ideas inherent from the beginning in the doctrines of the first English separatists is documented. Furthermore, the intellectural milieu from which Williams and his forerunners emerged is discussed, in so far as Williams was not an isolated figure, but part of a broader intellectual and religious tradition. In this manner, Williams is placed within the context of the English separatist tradition as representing an extreme position of complete differentiation between church and state.

Hundreds of volumes have been penned separately on Williams and on the separatists, including on the Pilgrim fathers and the first baptists (offshoots of the separatists), but no scholar has ever related Williams in a less than cursory manner to the English separatist tradition as a whole. True, Perry Miller, Edmund Morgan, and others have briefly noted that Williams was propelled by his uncompromising adherence to separatist principles, but no one has ever developed such ideas into a comprehensive thesis.

The second postulate is that Williams recast the theology of his spiritual forefathers into a new, more radical mode. Williams's teachings are declared to be a thorough reconstruction, rather than merely a restatement, of earlier doctrinal positions. As an uncompromising separatist, Williams went further in his quest for distinction than any separatist predecessor or contemporary. Compared with the precepts of all of the Elizabethan and Jacobean forerunners, Williams's biblically-based principle of complete church-state separation was revolutionary. In this light, the doctrinal positions of Williams are compared with those of his contemporaries and precursors in order to signify that his world view was an uncommon radicalization of and ideological extrapolation from the concept of "coming out" (i.e., of separating) developed six decades before by a few Tudor separatists.

Third, how religious separatism was transformed, as it crossed the Atlantic Ocean and was implanted in American soil, is discussed. After suffering much misunderstanding and persecution in England, separatism blossomed in the English colonies, becoming a potent, lively, and attractive force. Separation became an essential aspect of America, as witnessed by the growth and legitimacy of the denominational offspring of the separatist movement--the baptist and congregationalist churches. While there was a logical progression from old to new forms of nonconformity, in the New World the tenets of separatism differed significantly from those of its namesake in the motherland.

A fourth assertion is that separatist ecclesiology and political theory are best understood when viewed jointly. In old and New England during the early modern era, political implications were unavoidable since the institution from which the separatists sought to secede was a state church.

Government was expected to defend and enforce the true Christian faith. To challenge that arrangement was to commit treason as well as heresy. Political and religious factors were inextricably linked. Society was viewed, as it had been for centuries, as one Christian body or <u>corpus christianum</u>. The separatist claim to ecclesiastical freedom was implicitly a rejection of magisterial power and thus a political statement as well as a repudiation of the sacrosanct scheme of church-state unity. The separatists were perceived as seeking to limit the power of the monarch. They soon found themselves embroiled in more than a mere doctrinal or ecclesiastical dispute, even though they disavowed any desire for political power or attempts to establish a new world order. Internal ideological and spiritual concerns underlie much of the political agitation of the time, especially questions regarding obedience and liberty. Ecclesiastical dissent was necessarily political. Though the primary concern of the separatists was doctrinal and ecclesiastical, their challenge was necessarily political, rather than purely religious. Under the circumstances, they were labeled enemies of the state.

Finally, it is my contention that ideas, as well as economics and politics, determine history. Frequently, individuals and groups are motivated by the vision of a better world. Social change comes through the inspiration and teachings of religious leaders willing to condemn established systems and policies. Society benefits from the bold, provocative, and disruptive spirit of a genuine man of God and troubler of conscience. Fortunately, not everyone in a given age is as intemperate and uncompromising in pursuit of godly ideals as the true troubler of conscience, or consensus would be difficult to obtain. Immoderation is not always good, nor is it the only way to bring about constructive change. Nevertheless, the world needs religiously-inspired people of integrity, faith and fortitude motivated by noble ideals. When confronted with complacency, sin, and corruption, decisive leadership is required and may transcend (for the moment) conventional mores.

Today we live in an age which values moderation and is skeptical of fanaticism. Unfortunately, few people today realize the extent to which the great prophets and saints of the past contributed to human well-being and prosperity in large measure precisely because they were fanatical in their unbending commitment to certain God-centered principles of righteousness and justice. There is, in general, a time for everything, including uncompromising devotion to fixed principles and to a noble cause. When faced with social or religious injustice, society sometimes needs and benefits from righteous, public stands taken by people of conscience and conviction willing to state firmly their outrage with the standing order and their unwillingness to conduct business as usual. Often only extremists are able and willing to break through the barriers of convention to establish new patterns and perspectives.

Roger Williams was such an uncompromising zealot, an intellectual and social pioneer whose ideas deserve attention and understanding. The brashness and resoluteness of Williams's character made him a moving force in the American epic. By building on early separatist concerns, Williams was able to provide substantive theological reasons for what eventually became an essential aspect of the American way: free churches in a free society. Williams took the ecclesiological concepts of the English pioneers, expanded on those beliefs, and applied them to a newly emerging culture. Innovative and bold, Williams helped lay the groundwork for new approaches in politics as in religion. His theologically-based arguments eventually provided a clear path to civil tolerance and freedom for all, including Catholics, Moslems, and Jews.

Generally, Williams's roots within the English separatist tradition have been overshadowed by the polemical debate over the reasons for his banishment from Massachusetts in October 1635, by the influence and emotional appeal of his arguments on behalf of "soul liberty," and by his attack on the appropriation of Indian land on the basis of a royal patent. Ironically, Williams's expulsion can be understood fully only in light of his separatist heritage and the resultant opposition to the law of the land. Indeed, there is considerable circumstantial evidence to suggest that the theological debate over Massachusetts' policy of non-separatism triggered Williams's banishment. As Perry Miller pointed out in a cursory manner in Orthodoxy in Massachusetts, Massachusetts' policy of non-separatism was at the heart of the disagreement between Williams and the Bay colony during the early 1630s.[6] Williams was ousted because he openly preached dangerous ideas. That is to say, his disagreement was primarily doctrinal and only secondarily social. Williams challenged the accepted policy of state-imposed religious uniformity. Though prior to expulsion he disagreed with the puritan leaders of Massachusetts on a variety of specific ethical, legal, and social issues, none of those concerns should be considered in isolation from Williams's over-all separatist world view, especially his separatist-tinged ecclesiology and theory of church-state relations. Each altercation occurred on account of a fundamental difference of opinion which can only be understood within the context of an entire belief system, a consistent set of principles, espoused by all separatists. Williams's clashes with the authorities--over such concrete questions as the king's patent giving the settlers in Plymouth legal control over Indian land, an oath of loyalty to the General court of Massachusetts, cutting the cross out of the English flag, the veiling of women in church, letters against the churches in Massachusetts demanding separation (after an incident regarding land in Marblehead), rejection of communion with members of the Church of England and all other non-separatists, and denial of magisterial jurisdiction over religious affairs--occurred because of specific views advanced by Williams which were corollaries to a more basic set of separatist precepts which he accepted as axiomatic. The most important of those overriding tenets was a doctrine of separation that consisted of an unrelenting demand that civil and religious commitments be clearly differentiated and that magisterial power not be utilized to enforce religious conformity. His conviction was that the civil magistrate has no right to punish people for blasphemy, heresy, or any other breach of the first table of the Decalogue. Each specific issue was merely an outward manifestation of that fundamental view of life, as exemplified by Williams's opposition to an oath of civil allegiance and to the royal patent confiscating Indian land. Williams's insistence that an oath is something spiritual not to be employed by government as a civil instrument and that the English monarch (even if he is a regenerate Christian) has no divine right to take property from the heathens are precepts based on a doctrine of complete separation between religious and civil policy.

The reasons for Williams's banishment are debatable; however, the evidence indicates that he was expelled on account of a theological disagreement with the authorities over use of magisterial power to enforce religious conformity. Williams was forced to leave because of his insistence on complete separation of church and state--in light of a variety of positions which he espoused, based on separatism, regarding such specific issues as appropriation of Indian land and administration of a civil oath. Williams was not exiled due merely to a particular, isolated incident, but for rigid adherence to unorthodox theological principles. Williams's separatist ideology was manifested in a variety of different ways and resulted in various actions of nonconformity on his part. Nevertheless, those actions were not isolated occurences, but were consistent with his over-all ideological perspective.

It has long been believed that Williams was banished due to an attack on the royal patent and a defense of the Indians. But a reconstruction of the events makes it clear that such polemics were merely outgrowths of his separatist beliefs. Nor was Williams exiled because he advocated in the early 1630s liberty of conscience for all believers; his stress on individual rights and liberties was a natural outgrowth of his separatist world view that came about later. No reliable evidence exists that Williams advocated a full-blown doctrine of "soul liberty" prior to his literary debates with Cotton during the mid 1640s (i.e., several years after his expulsion). In an excellent recent study W. Clark Gilpin contends that a "fundamental shift [occurred] in Williams's theological position...between the years 1636 and 1643" which Gilpin attributes to "the adoption of a distinctive form of millenariaism."[7] Although Gilpin's explanation is disputable, during the years immediately succeeding his expulsion Williams seems to have experience a mental and emotional change. Apparently, he became disillusioned in his search for a perfect church. Williams searched so hard for a completely pure church that he became disenchanted when he did not find it. Realizing finally that the ideal of complete purity was unattainable, Williams reversed himself by advocating tolerance for people of all faiths. In the process, he moved from a concern with reformation to a focus on liberty and from intolerance to tolerance. In the final analysis, Williams determined that a pure church would not arrive until the second advent of Christ.

For Europe and America the seventeenth century was a religious age. Politics and religion were inextricably linked. To challenge the establishment in either England or New England was to commit heresy and sedition simultaneously. The insistence by the English separatists on freedom of worship, and by Roger Williams on civil justice for all, were necessarily political claims which were interpreted as implicit rejections of princely power. The separatists threatened both the orthodox faith and the standing social order by repudiating the widely-accepted principle of religious uniformity imposed by one official, national church.[8] From the beginning, the establishments in old and New England recognized the potential within separatism for divisiveness and for subversion. A dissident spiritual movement led by charismatic leaders represented a direct challenge to religious and political authority. As a result, those in power did not take the threat lightly.

The post-Reformation English state was erastian--the monarch governed the church as well as the state. The church was merely one among many divisions of the government. Priests were civil servants who owed their loyalty first to the state, second to the church. Laws regulating church affairs were enacted by Parliament and approved by the sovereign. The Act of Supremacy had made Elizabeth I "supreme governor" of the Church of England, even though she was not ordained. In that the state was supreme, the church was under civil authority. Organization, practices, policies, and creeds were subject to royal decree. Thus, in that Elizabeth was declared supreme head of the society of God on earth, the Tudor-Stuart state church system can be called erastian, even though it was not until the mid-seventeenth century that the term was widely used in England.[9]

The ecclesiastical situation in colonial Massachusetts was similar to that of England. In fact, since the clergy were politically influential, many historians have asserted that Massachusetts Bay was theocratic. Perry Miller called Massachusetts Bay a theocracy, and Alden Vaughan has written that at the very least it was "theocentric if not theocratic."[10] In 1942 Gaius Atkins and Frederick Fagley described the structure in early Massachusetts as a church-state system, rather than a state church arrangement as existed in England.[11] If the definition of a theocracy is that the clergy are either government officials or essentially determine public policy, puritan New England was not a theocracy, since the magistrates, rather than ministers, ruled. But insofar as a Christian theocracy is a society heavily influenced by clerics, Massachusetts Bay fits the description.

The magistrates and the clergy in Massachusetts both viewed civil government as an active instrument for spiritual as well as political control. They sought to build an ideal Christian community that would be a city upon a hill for other to imitate and many believed that their society was a New Israel. The duty of a civil magistrate, according to the leaders of Massachusetts as well as John Calvin, was to impose Christ's directives on the people. That role was threatened by separatism, especially by Williams's literal version of separation which challenged the essence of Massachusetts's standing order--its church-state system. The magistrates could hardly overlook such a menace. By attacking magisterial involvement in religious affairs, Williams presented the colonial establishment with an unwanted protest. Perceived as interfering with the colony's divinely-ordained mission as the New Israel, Williams's behavior was destined to incur political hostility.

Williams's radical ideas challenged the non-separatist policy of the colony on the Bay and provoked the ire of the authorities. To illustrate the point, John Cotton (the religious leader of Massachusetts Bay) told Williams in a letter that he was expelled "for ought I know, for your corrupt Doctrines [i.e., separatist principles], which tend to the disturbances both of civil and holy peace."[12] To have agreed to Williams's demands, Cotton and the other leaders would have had to deny the premise on which their society was built.

While the intent is not to delve into the entire history of separatism, it is instructive to study the lives and convictions of a few of the foremost separatists. To that end, the ecclesiological and political views of Roger Williams are compared with the precepts of three predecessors--Robert Browne, Henry Barrowe (c.1550-1593), and John Smyth--and two contemporaries--John Canne and John Clarke (1609-1676).

There were at least two eras in Anglo-American separatist history: from 1581 to 1620 and from 1620 to 1660. The first forty years was a formative period which saw the unsteady beginnings of English separatism under the inspired but erratic leadership of Robert Browne. Its growth was based on the courage and literary skills of the young barrister Henry

Barrowe. Its subsequent division into two parts (one baptist, the other non-baptist) was a result of the controversial self-baptism and theological transformation experienced by John Smyth. In 1581 Browne formed the first openly separatist congregation in the British Isles; in 1612 Smyth died and separatism splintered; and in 1620 the Pilgrim fathers landed in Plymouth, Massachusetts.

The second age ended in 1660 with the restoration of Charles II as the English monarch. Between 1620 and 1660 the separatist movement underwent a period of maturation. From 1620 until the late 1640s, the history of separatism is obscure; what little evidence exists indicates that the separatists were few in number and their congregations continued to be clandestine. Yet it was during this time that Williams converted to separatism; their activities in England prior to the outbreak of the English Civil War are largely unknown. After the execution of Charles I in 1649, however, the separatists in England became increasingly influential. During the troubled age of Oliver Cromwell (1599-1658), nonconformity in England emerged from the underground, flourished for the first time, and soon divided into a multitude of sects. Separatist thinking of the 1640s and '50s was more diverse and diffuse than the earlier unified variety of Browne, Barrowe, Robinson, and Brewster. This volume is concerned primarily with understanding Williams's middle years, his years as a controversialist from 1644 to 1652. In 1644 Williams issued in London (without the name of either author or publisher) his magnum opus, The Bloudy Tenent of Persecution, an eloquent plea for complete freedom of conscience and an attack on Massachusetts Bay congregationalism. By then he had become a staunch advocate of civil justice for all religious dissenters. In 1652 Williams penned The Bloody Tenent Yet More Bloody; it would be another twenty-four years before he would write another treatise.

Introduction

Endnotes

[1][Roger Williams], The Bloudy Tenent, of Persecution, for cause of Conscience, discussed, in a Conference betweene Truth and Peace . . . (London, 1644), ed. Samuel L. Caldwell, The Complete Writings of Roger Williams (New York,, 1963), III, 58; cited hereafter as Complete Writings.

In 1866 the Narragansett Club of Providence, Rhode Island published most of Williams's writings in a six volume set entitled The Writings of Roger Williams. In 1963 Russell & Russell published a seven volume set under the heading The Complete Writings of Roger Williams which consisted of a facsimile of the Narragansett edition plus a seventh volume, edited by Perry Miller, which included an interpretative essay and five tracts not included in the earlier collection. Williams's works will be cited from the Russell & Russell edition. The editor of each volume differed and is cited as that work is introduced.

Since 1963 three scholars have published reviews of the literature on Roger Williams: LeRoy Moore, Nancy E. Peace, and Edward W. Coyle. These three studies show that interpretations of Williams may be classified, chronologically, into six historical periods: (1) unsympathetic contemporary accounts by John Winthrop and William Bradford; (2) polemical attacks by such early American historians as Nathaniel Morton, William Hubbard, and Cotton Mather defending the leaders of Massachusetts Bay and depicting Williams as a troublemaker; (3) the works of such baptist scholars as Isaac Backus, John Callender, and James Knowles which perceived Williams as having fought for religious freedom against an authoritarian church-state system; (4) the romantic view of such twentieth century historians as Vernon Parrington, James Ernst, and Samuel Brockunier who envisioned Williams as a social democrat and as the forerunner of modern, secular liberalism; (5) the realistic perspective of Perry Miller, Edmund Morgan, and Mauro Calamandrei highlighting Williams's Calvinistic biblicism; and (6) recent studies by Alan Simpson, John Garrett, W. Clark Gilpin, and Sacvan Bercovitch which slightly modify some of Miller's and Morgan's work. For reviews of the Williams literature, see LeRoy Moore, "Roger Williams and the Historians," Church History, Vol. 332, No. 4 (Dec., 1963), 432-51; Nancy E. Peace, "Roger Williams--a Historiographical Essay," Rhode Island History, Vol. 35 (Nov., 1976), 3-13; and Edward W. Coyle, "From Sinner to Saint: A Study of the Critical Reputation of Roger Williams with an Annotated Bibliography of Writings About Him," Ph.D. dissertation, University of Massachusetts, 1974.

Methodologically, there have been four approaches to the life and thought of Williams: (1) analyses of Williams's theology by Garrett, Gilpin, Cyclone Covey, Philip Gura, Orvil Hunsaker, Perry Miller, Morgan, Simpson, William Miller, and Clarence Roddy, some of which relate Williams cursorily to separatist thought, though without interpreting Williams within the context of the entire separatist tradition; (2) examinations of Williams's political philosophy by Parrington, Ernst, and Brockunier which deemphasize his theology and therefore fail to present adequately his social philosophy; (3) literary analyses of Williams's writings by Bercovitch, Miller, Richard Reinitz, and Moses Tyler which highlight neither the theological nor the political content of his message; (4) biographical and historical works which have been written about Williams's early life, his banishment from Massachusetts, his role as a missionary, and his role in the founding and governing of Rhode Island without comparing his views with those of other separatists.

Excellent histories have been published on the dissenting religious tradition in England, including studies by Horton Davies, Leland Carlson, E. B. White, and Michael Watts, but few works have been written on the contribution of separatism to America. Robert Bartlett, John Demos, George Langdon, and others have written on the history of Plymouth colony; Richard Gildrie on Salem; and William McLoughlin on the baptists in America. A few people have written on Williams, but no one has ever highlighted Williams's separatism as the most decisive single element in interpreting his adult life and thought.

Unfortunately, secular and religious historians alike have viewed Williams generally from other, less central, perspectives. For his famous antagonist, John Cotton, Williams was a heretic. Hubbard viewed him as seeking to destroy the God-ordained commonwealth of Massachusetts. For Backus, Williams was America's first great apostle of religious liberty. Ernst and Brochunier perceived him primarily as a social democrat. In a brief biography written after World War II, Perry Miller contended Williams was primarily a Biblical typologist, even though during the 1930s in Orthodoxy in Massachusetts Miller acknowledged Williams's connection to the separatist tradition. Finally, Gilpin asserts that he is best understood as a pietistic millenarian. Each of these perspectives has a certain amount of validity, but they all miss the distinguishing factor in Williams's life of faith: Williams was primarily a separatist after 1631 and only secondarily something else. Even after Williams adopted a belief in believer's baptism in the late 1630s, he remained religiously a separatist.

Williams was simultaneously a rebel, a heretic, a controversialist, a millenarian, an apostle of soul liberty, a social democrat, and a religious visionary. Yet few historians have even acknowledged the most significant aspect of Williams's intellectual life: his commitment to separatism. The fundamental historiographical problem is that most scholars have been describing the consequences, but not the causes, of Williams's life and career. The separatist world view was the force that animated him to do what he did. To suggest a parallel: for a writer to ignore Williams's separatist view of life would be like a biographer neglecting to mention that Ronald Reagan was essentially a conservative Republican while serving as President of the United States.

[2]Soul liberty, a term coined by Williams, is the belief that an individual's conscience should be free of outside interference.

[3]Nathaniel B. Shurtleff, ed., Records of the Governor and Company of the Massachusetts Bay in New England (1628-86), 5 vols. (Boston, 1853-54), I, 160; hereafter Massachusetts Bay Records. Cf. [John Winthrop], Winthrop's Journal, 1630-1649 (Boston, 1649), ed. James K. Hosmer (New York, 1928), I, 154.

[4]Because there were degrees of separateness, there were both inflexible and moderate expressions of separatism within the same overall movement. Some separatists, like the Pilgrim pastor John Robinson, have been called semi-separatists because they were moderate compared with others (although B. R. White expressly denies Robinson's moderation), while in the 1630s Williams was known for his rigidity and unwillingness to compromise. The pejorative phrase "rigid separation" was employed by Williams's opponents to indicate the inflexibility of Williams's commitment to radical puritan beliefs. For instance, the official historian for Massachusetts Bay, William Hubbard, depicted Williams as adhering to the "principles of rigid separation." A contemporary of Williams, Hubbard vehemently defended the non-separatist establishment in that colony, presenting Williams as a troublemaker and heretic by referring to "the great and lamentable apostasy of Mr. Williams." See William Hubbard, A General History of New England from the Discover to MDCLXXX (Cambridge, 1680; Boston reprint, 1815), 204 and 202.

[5]William Bradford, History of Plymouth Plantation, 1620-1647, ed. Worthington C. Ford (Boston, 1912), I, 161.

[6]See Perry Miller, Orthodoxy in Massachusetts, 1630-1650 (Cambridge, 1933), 157-58.

[7]W. Clark Gilpin, The Millenarian Piety of Roger Williams (Chicago, 1979), 51

[8]From the point of view of the authorities the separatists appeared to be destroying the status quo, whereas their own view was that they were calling for restitution of the system that Christ first instituted.

[9]Thomas Liebler (1524-1583), known as Erastus, was a professor of medicine at Heidelberg and court physician to the Elector Palatine. A follower of the Swiss reformer Ulrich Zwingli (1484-1531), he opposed giving power to the elders to excommunicate people without permission of the ruler. The Erastian party which emerged in England in 1643 during the Westminster Assembly in opposition to the Presbyterians denied any autonomy to the church apart from the government.

[10]Alden Vaughan, ed., The Puritan Tradition in America 1620-1730 (New York, 1972), 147.

[11]Gaius G. Atkins and Frederick L. Fagley, The History of American Congregationalism (Boston, 1942), 80.

[12]John Cotton, A Letter of Mr. John Cottons Teacher of the Church in Boston, in Nevv-England, to Mr Williams a Preacher there (London, 1643), ed. Reuben A. Guild, Complete Writings, I, 334.

CHAPTER I

SEPARATISM DELINEATED

In England during the late sixteenth century the comprehensive reformation sought by the puritans was stymied by Queen Elizabeth's insistence on a policy of via media. The most extreme of the puritans reacted to the failure to achieve complete reform by rebelling openly against the established system and by seeking extra-constitutional means to achieve their ends. As a result, during the 1580s Tudor puritanism divided into two camps on the question of the proper way to achieve further change.[1] Under the circumstances, one group--the moderate wing--conformed, refusing to abandon the Church of England. They considered themselves devote Anglicans and sought change only through official channels.[2] The second camp--the radical wing--was a tiny but troublesome minority of thoroughgoing or "forward" puritans who condemned the Anglican Church as utterly corrupt. Convinced that it was no longer possible to achieve reform through the status quo, they left the official state church to set up an alternative system of clandestine, religious conventicles. Because they dissociated completely from the all inclusive mother church, they were dubbed "separatists." Though small in number, they were an historically significant group. Originally, they were called "Brownists," after Robert Browne, the first avid English separatist. However, since Brownism commonly connoted sedition, most subsequent separatists denied the label.

Impatient with governmental procrastination and control, and willing to defy the authorities, the English separatists broke completely with the one national church. They took literally St. Paul's directive in II Corinthians 6:17 to "come ye out from among them and separate yourselves saith the Lord." It was a drastic step, but the separatists were no longer disposed to wait for officially-sanctioned change. They wanted to carry out the Protestant Reformation immediately "without tarying for anie."[3] They believed that ecclesiastical reformation should take place apart from any human decisions, including the edicts of the crown.

The first separatists are important, among other reasons, because they were the first in England to highlight the autonomy of each local church body and to adopt a congregational form of church organization. The separatists believed that congregationalism was in accord with the true apostolic model, and distinct from the ministerial, liturgical, and governmental system of the Church of England.

In contrast, most puritans saw religious uniformity enforced through one official church as essential to truth. The majority were social conservatives or practical moderates who upheld the view that there should be only one church in any given sovereignty (as long as the sovereign was Protestant). In time they became known as "non-separatists." Yet, the non-separatists are not easily understood, because inherent within their views are contradictions. On the one hand, they espoused the view that the state-supported church required purification to be true, while simultaneously refusing to repudiate the Anglican establishment and its practices. Because the non-separatists viewed separation as ecclesiastically divisive and politically seditious, they sought accommodation with those in power and denounced separation as contrary to the Christian tradition and to English civil law.

It would be impossible to describe either the separatists or non-separatists in absolute terms since the boundaries of belief are by no means clear-cut. Originally, both were puritans, differing in strategy but in neither objective nor creed. Nonetheless, at the point at which further reform seemed unlikely, the moderates conformed (at least overtly) and the radicals rebelled.[4]

Ecclesiology, as an issue in modern intellectual history, deserves more attention than it has received. Indeed, the doctrine of the church is at the heart of the separatist world view because of the importance radical puritans placed on the notion of a voluntary church structure. Obsessed with questions of order, separatists believed that polity was an essential aspect of church life and doctrine. This concern was observed by William Haller who noted that during the seventeenth century most English sects were "from the start preoccupied with the problem of organization.[5] To illustrate further: the Pilgrim pastor John Robinson explained that "the order which Christ hath left in the Evangelists, Act, and Epistles to Timothy and Titus is a part of the Gospel and the object of faith as much as any other part of it."[6]

Episcopacy, presbyterianism, and congregationalism are three different types of church polity. The majority of puritans in the late sixteenth and early seventeenth centuries favored either episcopacy or presbyterianism. Episcopacy, as a system of church government, consists of a superior order of clergy known as bishops who act as overseers, whereas presbyterianism is a representative ecclesiastical system comprised of assemblies of presbyters or elders.

However, disillusionment with the status quo caused the separatists to reject both systems and to develop a voluntaristic form of government: congregationalism. Congregationalism accentuates the independence of each local church body. As John Smyth expressed it, "Every visible church is of equal power with all other visible churches.[7] As such, congregationalism lacks a sense of catholicity. Designed only for the visible saints, it makes little allowance for the non-elect. Only those who freely choose to join a church truly belong.

Congregationalism is a distinguishing feature of Anglo-American separatism. Edmund Morgan, for example, has observed that the English separatists were "the first Puritans to practice what was later called Congregationalism."[8] The separatists believed it to be the polity of first-century Christianity and thus divinely ordained. Congregationalism is a decentralized system in which the local congregation is viewed as the basic ecclesiastical unit. Congregationalism, as advocated in its pure form by the separatists, rejects any coercive authority in matters of faith, including synods or presbyters, since it is based on the principle of voluntarism.

Dogmatically, Barrowe declared it inconceivable that "these blasphemous wretches" (i.e., the bishops) believed that "the true church of Christ may take another order of government" than congregationalism.[9]

According to separatist thinking, the local church is sovereign over its membership, its liturgy, its ceremonies, exercise of discipline, employment of ministers, election of officers, and utilization of property, and a real church need be only a large as a single congregation. The biblical understanding of polity is congregational; each local religious community is self-governing unit and possesses all ecclesiastical power. The true church is free of national standards and controls. A local church cannot and should not be coerced by kings, bishops, courts, or synods. "There is no king of the church but Christ," professed the Pilgrim father, John Robinson.[10] This view has been dubbed "the crown rights of the Redeemer" doctrine. As a principle of organization it has allowed sectarianism, in time, to flourish.

Separatists, like the presbyterians, believed that the New Testament provided specific guidelines for church government. Because they believed congregationalism was the organization of Christ as revealed in the scriptures, separatists modeled their churches only after that specific apostolic pattern, rejecting all other polities as false and unchristian. The separatists were ecclesiological and political restitutionists who sought to imitate the primitive Christian ideal of "particular churches." In his writings, Roger Williams concurred with other separatists, saying that only particular churches are in accord with the true apostolic model. [11] God's desire was to call "his people more and more out of the Babel of confused Worships, Ministries, & c [sic]." "The church is built," Williams wrote in The Bloudy Tenent of Persecution, "upon the foundation of the Apostles and Prophets."[12] Rhetorically, Williams asked New England's most famous preacher and his principal antagonist, John Cotton (1584-1652), "if the Lord Jesus were himself in person in old or New England, what Church, what Ministry, what Worship, what Government would he set up, and what persecution would he practice toward them that would not receive Him?"[13] For Williams the answer to the first question was particular congregations; to the second, Christ renounced persecution.

For the English separatists a church is a voluntary association of Christian believers worshipping in accord with the apostolic pattern characterized by a covenant, an elect membership, a congregational polity, freedom from state control, and independence from outside authority.[14] To

Browne and Barrowe the church consists only of saints; moreover, it is defined on the basis of the faith and conduct of its members rather than geographical or hierarchical considerations.

The term "congregationalist" denotes those Stuart churchmen who held to a semi-separatist stand. On the one hand, in theory, congregationalists believed in the congregational form of church government while alternatively, in practice, they opposed separatism.[15] During the 1640s in England, puritan advocates of congregationalism acquired the name "Independents," and in America they were initially dubbed as exponents of "the New England Way," yet the word congregationalist seems to be the best and simplest expression. Dr. William Ames was the principal theologian of puritan congregationalism; Henry Jacob (1563-1624) its instigator in England; and Williams's literary opponent and antagonist, John Cotton, its chief spokesman in America. Most likely it was Cotton who coined the expression congregationalism. The Keyes of the Kingdom of Heaven, composed in 1644, is Cotton's primary defense of the principles of non-separating congregationalism. During the Westminster Assembly of Divines (1643-46), a group of five Independent clergy allied ideologically with Cotton--known as the five "Dissenting Brethren"--expressed the same views a few months later in a tract titled the Apologeticall Narration. Four years later in Massachusetts the Cambridge Platform, which included a preface written by Cotton, codified the principles of non-separating congregationalism into law. Nineteenth-century Congregational historian Williston Walker called this "the most important monument of early New England Congregationalism."[16]

According to Perry Miller, non-separating congregationalists were "anti-Separatists...[who] quietly accepted the Separatists' discipline."[17] Publicly non-separatists were opposed to separatism, however, in reality their system of church government bore remarkable resemblance to that of the separatists, especially in America where sharp distinctions were seldom drawn. Congregationalism or Independency was a conservative expression of many of the same schismatic precepts found in more radical form among the brethren of the separation. Except in the realm of political thought,distinctions between separatists and congregationalists, including those between Williams and Cotton, were political and tactical, not doctrinal. True, there was a degree of disparity regarding church polity and other ecclesiastical as well as political areas, but most differences had more to do with strategy, politics, and methodology than with theology, ecclesiastical practice, and goals. In theory there were divergences, in practice there were few, indicating that theological positions were employed, possibly subconsciously, to justify other strategic or political positions. It is probably that Ames sought to set up a voluntary system of church government within the overall parish system of the Ecclesia Anglicana because he wanted to lend credibility and respectability to the new organizational plan.

Congregationalists and separatists emerged from the same common doctrinal ground, yet differed in attitudes toward ecclesiastical supervision and toward the official state church. As to supervision, congregationalists acknowledged the right of occasional advisory synods and of other independent churches to exercise supervision over each local church in spite of the belief in the autonomy of each congregation. With regard to the Church of England, when compelled to make a choice, congregationalists conformed and separatists rebelled. Unlike the separatists, paradoxically the congregationalists sought to maintain a commitment concurrently to two contradictory ideals: state-enforced religious uniformity and congregational autonomy based on the gathering of visible saints. The separatists adhered only to the latter doctrine.

While Williams's debate with Cotton regarding religious liberty is mentioned only briefly in this work, a brief discussion of ecclesiological and political differences between these two antagonists is in order. Even though Williams and Cotton were in basic agreement on most doctrinal issues, the polemical disparity was sharp and incongruities abound in their respective understandings of the need for synods, church-state cooperation, magisterial involvement in spiritual affairs, and liberty of conscience. Without a doubt Cotton was not a separatist. In Keyes of the Kingdom he characterized the New England Way as a middle way between separatism and presbyterianism.[18] Williams sought to demonstrate just as ardently that the system in Massachusetts was inherently intolerant.

Cotton and Williams were great men, yet neither of them was able to see either his opponent or himself objectively. In spite of a common starting point within the same puritan tradition, they represented two different ways of looking at the relationship between religion and culture. Accordingly, they arrived at different answers to the same problem. Unfortunately, Williams tended to perceive Cotton as a hypocritical dictator, rather than as the moderate diplomat he was, while Cotton viewed Williams as a self-righteous fanatic, instead of as a straightforward visionary. The conflict between them was in response to corruption within the Anglican church. Initially, it was because the English system failed to work properly that they each crossed the Atlantic Ocean to find the true church of God. But Williams and Cotton experienced a distinct generation gap. Williams was nearly twenty years younger than Cotton, and thus understandably less aware of political and diplomatic realities and more concerned with spiritual ideals. In England Cotton was a well-known puritan preacher while Williams was a youngster. The youthful Williams reached the peak of his idealistic yearning and enthusiasm soon after arriving in Massachusetts; he later mellowed as he approached middle age.

In general, separatists and non-separatists differed in three or more ways: in their understanding of the ministry, church polity, forms of worship, standards of membership, and the authority of ecclesiastical officials; strategically as to how best to bring about the puritan idea (e.g., by active or passive resistance); and politically in their view of the proper relationship between church and state and in their attitude toward civil authority. Even so, it is important to note that congregationalists and separatists varied only slightly regarding ecclesiastical theory and practice.[19] Unlike Anglicans and presbyterians, congregationalists adopted most aspects of separatist ecclesiology. For instance, Cotton accepted the separatist definition of a church as an autonomous congregation composed of visible saints while retaining paradoxically the medieval principle of state-enforced religious uniformity.

Ecclesiological Differences

Throughout Christian history there have been various groups, usually sects, which have sought to purify the Church by sifting the wheat (the saints) from the tares (the wicked or hypocritical). Many Christians, besides the English separatists, have been concerned with questions of purification. Christ's parable of the wheat and the tares in 13 Matthew 24-27 has been variously interpreted. Williams employed that famous allegory as a proof-text for religious liberty.[20] During the fourth century, St. Augustine (354-430) accused the Donatists of heresy on the grounds that only God knows who is elect. For Christianity, the question of wheat and tares has been a recurring issue.

The English separatists sought to establish churches without spot or wrinkle--composed only of visible saints. They believed they were able to maintain true and stable churches only by excluding those who do not conform to rigorous standards of discipline. As Henry Barrowe noted from a prison cell, "What a preposterous dealing is this, to receave the wicked unto the Lordes table.... This is cleane contrary to the apostles doctrine."[21] Even though the early separatists denied belief in human perfectibility, their goal nevertheless was to erect morally pure communities.[22] The separatists were convinced that a true Christian church consists only of those who can demonstrate election conclusively. According to Browne:

> No wickednesse is tolerable. . . . Knowe ye not (saith the Scripture) that a little leaueneth the whole lumpe. . . . Howe then dare these menne [Anglicans] teache vs that anie euill thing is tolerable in the Church, as though the church gouernement could not remedie it: yea and so tolerable, that all men should be brought into bondage thereby.[23]

Cotton and the advocates of the New England Way adopted the separatist discipline and exhibited certain separatist characteristics, yet their stress on religious conformity places them primarily with the non-separatists. Cotton's view was that "the field" in Christ's parable was the church and "the tares" were church members who were either moral offenders or hypocrites. He believed that (since hypocrites cannot be excommunicated without removing some of the truly regenerate) non-elect Christians should be allowed to remain members of the church; there is thus no reason to uproot the tares since they will be destroyed with the advent of Christ at the time of the final "harvest" (i.e., on the Day of Judgment). It is difficult, Cotton taught, for men but not for God to distinguish between the wheat of truth and the tares of heresy. In contrast, Williams contended that the field was the world or civil government rather than the church and that the tares were unregenerate or evil people who have no right to be church members, not merely hypocritical Christians. He contended that it was possible to determine who the offenders are and believed they should be removed at the present moment rather than after Christ's return. Christians and non-believers are to exist side-by-side, but separated, until the end of the world. "Hypocrites were not," wrote Williams, "intended by the Lord Jesus in this famous Parable."[24] "The command of Christ Jesus . . . [was] to permit the tares to grow in the field of the world," but not in the church.[25] Cotton agreed that the field may be the world, but he contended it was the church scattered around the planet rather than the earth's entire population. In contradistinction, Browne and Robinson (like Cotton) had taught that "by tares in the field are meant not notorious offenders, but hypocrites."[26]

Williams's and Cotton's exegesis of the parable in Matthew is significant for a variety of reasons, including the light it sheds on the doctrines of liberty and tolerance. For Williams, the parable is no longer merely a question of church discipline; it is also an argument against use of civil authority to enforce religious doctrines and practices. He believed in strict discipline for those within the church, including the weeding out of hypocrites, but argued for liberality toward all those outside. On the other hand, Cotton favored the imposition of religious conformity on all and a broad-based state church encompassing the entire population. The tares, he argued, should be allowed to grow freely among the wheat until the day when Christ returns to judge the quick and the dead.

In response to the Donatist movement of the fourth century, Augustine developed a doctrine of two churches--one visible, the other invisible. The former consists of all baptized members and is the empirical, institutional ecclesiastical association upon earth, the latter is composed only of the elect and is the unknown spiritual group of true Christian believers. The Donatists compelled Augustine to formulate his ecclesiology explicitly. For him the catholicity of the church is assumed, but his teachings have been variously understood. Radicals and conservatives asserted they were in accord with the orthodox Augustinian view. Whereas most radicals have sought to reduce the gap between the two types of churches, conservatives have tended to highlight the distinction.[27] Augustine, and most of the Protestant reformers, asserted the ultimately only God knows who is a true Christian. In theory, most radicals accepted this epistemological restraint on human knowledge; but in practice, few did. Through rigid standards of membership and disciplinary measures, most of them sought to correlate the visible and invisible church and thus, in effect, judge others. English separatists generally held to literal interpretations of Augustinian doctrine. To cite an instance, Barrowe wrote that "God hath set downe the whole processe and due time and maner of sentence thereof [in the Bible]: he hath left nothin therein to the discretion of the church."[28] On this point, Williams upheld a more extreme view than the original English separatists, by repudiating the Augustinian distinction between the visible and invisible church completely and by rejecting the possibility of a pure church until the Last Days.

Strategic Divergences

While controversy between separatists and non-separatists centered theologically on the doctrine of the church, in practice their disagreements were tactical: how best to achieve the puritan idea. Though at times they may have sympathized with the Brownist cause, most puritan divines disapproved of secessionist tactics. Non-separatists viewed such "coming out" from a pragmatic perspective, seeing it as a threat to the credibility of and potential for the entire puritan movement. They believed that radical approaches cast aspersions on the legitimacy of their own efforts to achieve reform, so they were unwilling to support separatism publicly. Certainly these conservative puritan reformers were not conformists, but neither were they dissidents. They wanted to reconstitute existing institutions, not erect new ones. The non-separatists recognized imperfections within the established Church, but did not demand instant reform. They shared with their radical brethren the desire for purification but were more prudent and seemingly more tolerant. Moreover, they feared the fragmentation of the body of Christ that they predicted would result from sectarianism--often seeming more concerned with unity than holiness. Alarmed by the separatist tendency toward liberty, they perceived Browne in Tudor England and Williams in colonial New England as dangerous schismatics.

It is important to remember that the non-separatists were convinced that separatism was ill conceived and ineffective. They were concerned with issues of heresy and sedition, not rights and liberties. Although it is true that to be branded a separatist was to be hated and rejected, most non-separatist leaders probably were cautious, not cowardly. The non-separatist leaders probably were cautious, not cowardly. The non-separatists sought to fight the battle for righteousness within church and society. Though faced with difficulties, they were confident they could win the entire nation, including the church hierarchy, to their cause. Indeed, during the Cromwellian protectorate a form of non-separating puritanism temporarily gained ascendancy. Of course, at the beginning of the seventeenth century this pragmatic approach was also more respectable--and resulted in less suffering, as Williams pointed out.[29] But personal safety was probably not a prime motive. Ideologically they were, within the spectrum of puritanism, authentic moderates.[30] Williams, however, implied in 1644 in Mr. Cottons Letter Lately Printed, Examined and Ansvvered that it was out of "fear of persecution or otherwise" that the Massachusetts leaders decided not to practice the separation in which they believed.[31]

Separatists abhorred moderation, dubbed by Williams "middle walking." In matters of principle, they opposed compromise since "scripture only must be heard."[32] Several examples will illustrate the sectarian position. During questioning by several clergymen prior to his execution, Barrowe criticized Thomas Cartwright (1535-1603), the leader of the proto-presbyterian movement, for his unwillingness to proceed wholeheartedly with the reformation: "I cannot but complaine of Maister Cartwright and others of his knowledge (opinion), from whom we have received the truth of these things, (by whose books we) have been taught, that your callings are antichristian; who yet utterly, against their consciences, forsake us in our sufferings."[33] When the puritan minister Richard Bernard, who himself had once been a separatist, attempted (from an Anglican perspective) to defend a midway position between "the schismaticall Brownists" and "the Antichristian Papists," Robinson responded by comparing such a view with the tragic experiences of the ancient Israelites when they found themselves caught midway between God and Baal.[34]   Likewise, Williams accused Cotton and the leaders in Massachussetts of walking "between Christ and Antichrist."[35] "With the Lord's gracious assistance," declared Williams, "we shall prove this middle walking to be less than halting."[36]   The separatists charged the moderates with being inconsistent in that they failed to apply the same standards to Canterbury they had applied to Rome.   If Protestants were justified in seceding from the papacy because it was corrupt (hence, false), it was their duty to separate from the Anglican system of monarchical episcopacy for the same reason.   To be logical, all puritans must denounce both.[37]   Thus, Williams (like his contemporary separatist, John Canne) advocated "the unavoidable conclusions of the nonconformists' principles."[38]

Mainstream puritans, like Cartwright, disagreed; they denied the separatist premise that Christ's ideal was based on congregational or independent principles and that the Church of England was thus false.   In response to the charge of inconsistency, non-separating congregationalists as well as presbyterians asserted that the logic of their arguments compelled conversion, not abandonment, of the entire church.   Non-separatists averred that they were carrying Calvinism to its final conclusion and saw no need to go further.   For them, the Anglican Reformation was divinely ordained.[39]

Political Differences

Attitudes toward the Ecclesia Anglicana also differed.   Whereas most puritans refused to challenge in a fundamental manner the system of church-state cooperation, the separatists did.   Assured that religion should not be unduly subject to political control, several generations of dissenters denounced civil supremacy over religious affairs.

Browne relied on proof-texts from the Old Testament to justify his position in his major work, Reformation without Tarying:

> We knowe that Moses might reforme, and the iudges and
> Kings which followed him, and so may our Magistrates. . . .
> Yet may they doo nothing concerning the Church, but onelie
> ciuilie, and as ciuile Magistrates, that is, they haue not that
> authoritie ouer the Church, as to be Prophetes or Priestes, or
> spiritual Kings. . . . but onelie to rule the common wealth in all
> outward Iustice.[40]

Interestingly, Browne's use of the Old Testament anticipated Cotton's view rather than that of Williams whose brand of separatism was New Testament-oriented. Barrowe, too, believed that English law should conform to Mosaic law, whereas Williams took the opposite view that the law of Israel no longer applied.

For separatists, the regnum itself is subject to discipline, including excommunication, even though this was contrary to the role of the monarch established by law. Browne and Barrowe both maintained this position. In a 1592 tract Barrowe wrote that "the prynce for anie transgression of God's lawes is liable and subjecte to the censures and judgementes of Christe in his churches, which are withowte partialitie or respecte of persones".[41] Barrowe commented further:

> O how great is the blindnes of these phariseis when they give unto princes such blasphemous titles, popish prerogative and dispensations, as SUPREME HEAD OF THE CHURCH. . ., yet is it still the censure and judgment of Christ, unto which every servant of Christ and member of the Church must be subject [including the monarch].[42]

Barrowe warned the establishment in 1592, "That nation or common wealth, prince, magistrate. . . person, whosoever that submitteth not to our Lord Jesus Christ to be wholy governed by his word both bodie and soule in al things whatsoever without anie exception. . .shall be utterlie destroyed amongst Christ's enemies."[43] The separatists were among the first to deny use of civil law and authority to punish heresy or moral sin. In so doing, they threatened the foundation of post-Reformation England--its erastian system of civil supremacy over religious affairs.

The Brownists and Barrowists refused to render to Caesar that which is God's. They questioned the authority of the monarch, refusing to recognize the queen, who was by law supreme governor of the church, as head of their congregations.[44] Nineteenth-century Congregational historian Henry Dexter contended in The Congregationalism of the Last Three Hundred Years that the English separatists were the first to defend the now widely accepted belief that political jurisdiction over religious activity should be limited.[45] By challenging the government's monopoly on religion, the radicals threatened the crown's right to absolute power. For instance, in

Briefe Discoverie Barrowe commented, "Most willing they are with al their people to remaine in spiritual bondage to the civil magistrate. (I would not here be misunderstood of that lawful bodily obedience which al Christians owe in al lawful things unto the civil magistrate.)"[46]

By dissociating from the state church, and hence from government control, the separatists paved the way for the modern notion of clear distinctions between the functions of church and state.[47] While it would be misleading to state that the sectarians alone discovered the modern concept, the ideas they promulgated were a contributing factor. They provided new approaches to questions regarding relationships between religion and politics. Even though they did not believe in the modern principle of separation, the separatists were convinced that religious concerns were solely spiritual and should not be corrupted by worldly affairs, and that it is wrong for civil officials to interfere in ecclesiastical affairs. Robinson insisted that "as the 'kingdom of Christ is not of this world,' John 28:36, but spiritual, and he a spiritual king; so must the government of this spiritual kingdom, under this spiritual king, needs to be spiritual, and all the laws of it."[48] "My kingdome, saith Christe, is not of this world, and they [the Anglicans] would shift in both Bishopes and Magistrates into his spiritual throne to make it of this worlde," declared Browne in his principal tract on church-state relations, A Treatise of Reformation without Tarying for Anie.[49] The modern doctrine evolved over several centuries, the result of a variety of forces, including the dissident religious movement known as separatism. Though Williams's concern was to free religion from civil control, implicitly he and his cohorts helped to liberate the state from spiritual control also. The first English separatists wanted freedom for their own churches, but inadvertently also gained liberty for government as well.

This is not to argue that the early separatists were social insurrectionists. Unlike such sects of the 1640s as the Fifth Monarchists, Levellers, and Diggers, they never sought to overthrow the crown. Except for a few radicals such as Robert Harrison, they neither advocated nor resorted to use of force to gain power. Indeed, in 1610 Robinson wrote that authority "is to be obeyed in all things if they be good, actively, and by doing them; if evil and unlawful, passively and by suffering with meekness for righteousness sake, if pardon cannot be obtained."[50] Though seemingly unaware of the political overtones of their doctrine and actions, the early separatists never uttered a word about organizing an armed rebellion or conspiracy against the queen. The same cannot be said about some of Williams's separatist contemporaries, most notably John Canne and the Fifth Monarchists. Even Williams supported Cromwell and the Parliamentary rebellion. The early separatists may have had considerable resentment against the crown, but they never criticized political authority per se. Their attacks were directed against the system's control over their lives and congregations, not tolerance for others.

In the early modern world, political and religious institutions and factors were inextricably linked. To challenge the establishment in either England or New England was to commit heresy and sedition simultaneously. The insistence by the early separatists on ecclesiastical freedom and by Roger Williams on liberty of conscience were necessarily political claims which were interpreted as rejections of princely power. By repudiating the widely-accepted principle of religious uniformity, the separatists threatened the orthodox Anglican faith and the standing social order.[51] From the first tremors, the establishments in old and New England recognized the potential within separatism for divisiveness and for subversion. A new religious movement led by charismatic leaders represented a direct challenge to all existing authority. As a result, those in power did not take the threat lightly.

The political and religious authorities of Massachusetts viewed civil government as an active instrument for spiritual as well as political control. The duty of a civil magistrate, according to John Calvin and most early modern Christians, was to impose Christ's directives on the people. That role was threatened by separatism, especially by Williams's literal version of separation which challenged the essence of Massachusetts's standing order-- its church-state system. The magistrates could hardly overlook such a menace. By attacking magisterial involvement in religious affairs, Williams presented the colonial establishment with an unwanted protest. Perceived as interfering with the colony's divinely-ordained mission, Williams's public pronouncements were destined to incur political hostility.

Chapter 1

Endnotes

[1]Although the majority of people were Anglican, the separatists and the non-separating presbyterians emerged at that time, whereas the baptists and the non-separating congregationalist did not appear until the seventeenth century.

[2]While the contention that any puritan can be called temperate is debatable, presbyterians were more moderate than separatists in that they opposed separation.

[3]"Without tarying for anie," i.e., the belief that true believers should not wait for the entire church to be formed, is Robert Browne's famous declaration of independence from the Church of England. See Robert Browne, A Treatise of Reformation without Tarying for Anie, and of the Wickednesse of those Preachers which will not reforme till the Magistrate commaunde or compell them (Middelburg, 1582), ed. Albert Peel and Leland H. Carlson, The Writings of Robert Harrison and Robert Browne (London, 1953), 150-70, especially 154, 156, and 167 (hereafter Writings of Harrison and Browne).

[4]Secondary works that are helpful in distinguishing between separatism and non-separatism are Patrick Collinson, The Elizabethan Puritan Movement (Berkeley, 1967); Horton Davies, The Worship of the English Puritans (London, 1948), 77-78; Horton Davies, Worship and Theology in England (Princeton, 1970), I, xviii and 44; Marshall M. Knappen, Tudor Puritanism: A Chapter in the History of Idealism (Chicago, 1939); Perry Miller, Orthodoxy in Massachusetts 1630-1650 (Cambridge, Massachusetts, 1933), 53-101; Edmund Morgan, Visible Saints: The History of a Puritan Idea (Ithaca, 1963),, 17-20; Michael R. Watts, The Dissenters: From the Reformation to the French Revolution (Oxford, 1978), 28-30; and B. R. White, The English Separatist Tradition: From the Marian Martyrs to the Pilgrim Fathers (London, 1971), passim.

[5]Haller, 179.

[6]John Robinson, A Just and Necessarie Apologie of Certain Christians no less contumeliously than commonly called Brownists or Barrowists (Leyden, 1619), ed. Ashton, Works, III, 22.

[7]John Smyth, The Differences of the Churches of the Seperation: Contayning, a Description of the Leitovrgie and Ministerie of the Visible Church (Amsterdam, 1608), ed. W. T. Whitley, The Works of John Smyth: Fellow of Christ's College 1594-8 (Cambridge, England, 1915), I, 279 (hereafter Works of John Smyth). See also Browne, Reformation without Tarying, ed. Peel and Carlson, Writings, I, 150-55.

[8]Morgan, Visible Saints, 34.

[9]Henry Barrowe, A Briefe Discoverie of the False Church (Dort, 1592), ed. Leland H. Carlson, The Writings of Henry Barrow, 1587-90 (London, 1962), III, 555.

[10]John Robinson, A Justification of Separation from the Church of England against Mr. Richard Bernard his invective entitled the Separatists' Schism (Leyden, 1610), ed. Robert Ashton, The Works of John Robinson, Pastor of the Pilgrim Fathers (London, 1851), II, 31 (hereafter Works).

[11]Roger Williams, Mr. Cottons Letter Lately Printed, Examined and Ansvvered (London, 1644), ed. Reuben A. Guild, Complete Writings, I, 326-27; and Williams, The Bloudy Tenent, of Persecution, for cause of Conscience, ed. Caldwell, Complete Writings, III, 71-73.

[12]Roger Williams, The Hireling Ministry None of Christs, or a Discourse touching the Propagating the Gospel of Christ Jesus (London, 1652), ed. Perry Miller, Complete Writings, VII, 169; and Williams, Bloudy Tenent, ed. Caldwell, Complete Writings, III, 65.

[13]Roger Williams, Mr. Cottons Letter Lately Printed, Examined and Answered: By Roger Williams of Providence in New-England, ed. Reuben A. Guild, Complete Writings, I, 112.

[14]See Henry Barrowe, A True Description out of the Worde of God, of the Visible Church ([Dort], 1589), ed. Leland H. Carlson, The Writings of Henry Barrow, 1587-90 (London, 1958), III, 214; John Robinson, Of Religious Communion, private and public. With the silencing of the Clamours raised by Mr. Thomas Helwys against our retaining the baptism received in England, and administering of baptism unto infants (Leyden, 1614), ed. Ashton, Works, II, 132; and John Smyth, Principles and Inferences Concerning the Visible Church (Amsterdam, 1607), ed. Whitley, Works of John Smyth, I, 258.

[15]In this volume separating congregationalists are referred to as separatists and non-separating congregationalists are called congregationalists, albeit initially the latter were referred to in America as advocates of the New England Way and in England as Independents.

Although Champlin Burrage was the first scholar to observe the difference between separating and non-separating congregationalism, Perry Miller was the first to identify the non-separating congregationalists as a distinct group and to explain the theological views of such congregationalists as Dr. Williams Ames (1576-1633) and John Cotton. Prior to popularization of the Burrage-Miller thesis, most scholars differentiated clearly only between separating and non-separating puritanism, but did not delineate distinctions within congregationalism itself. In any case, today it is widely accepted that non-separating congregationalism was originally formulated by Ames at the turn of the century and put into practice by Cotton and the clergy of Massachusetts during the 1630s.

The seventeenth century Presbyterian divine Robert Baillie claimed all independents were separatists, denying the distinction between separating and non-separating congregationalism. In 1645 in A Dissuasive from the Errours of the Time Baillie declared that Cotton's views were synonymous with Brownism and that Brownism was the as continental anabaptism. Apparently Baillie was unaware of a middle way between presbyterianism and separatism--an oversight which is not surprising since it was not until the present century that historians were able to clarify subtle differences between the positions.

[16]Williston Walker, The Creeds and Platforms of Congregationalism (New York, 1893), 185. The official name of the Cambridge Platform is A Platform of Church Discipline Gathered Out of the Word of God and Agreed upon by the Elders and Messengers of the Churches Assembled in the Synod at Cambridge in New England (Cambridge, Massachusetts, 1648).
  The five Dissenting Brethren were Thomas Goodwin, Philip Nye, Sidrach Simpson, Jeremiah Burroughes, and William Bridge. They led the opposition in the Westminster Assembly to presbyterianism. They co-authored An Apologeticall Narration, Humbly Submitted to the Honourable Houses of Parliament (London, 1643). See Berndt Gustafsson, The Five Dissenting Brethren: A Study on the Dutch Background of their Independentism (Lund, 1955).

[17]Miller, Orthodoxy, 75.

[18]John Cotton, The Keyes of the Kingdom of Heaven (London, 1644), 18. See also Everett Emerson, Cotton, 70.

[19]For examples of ecclesiological divergences, see either Horton Davies, Worship and Theology, I, 325-26 or Gerald R. Cragg, Freedom and Authority: A Study of English Thought in the Early Seventeenth Century (Philadelphia, 1975), 219. For a discussion of the similarities, see Edmund Morgan, 6, 23, and 33; and William Bartlett, The Pilgrim Way, 133-35.
  Repudiating separation from the Church of England, William Ames and Henry Jacob argued (somewhat inconsistently) that the Anglican system of parishes should allow local congregations autonomy but not be based on voluntary gatherings. Ames's Marrow of Sacred Theology was read widely in America as well as in England.

[20]This dichotomization about Christian history is based primarily on Edmund Morgan's book Visible Saints. See Morgan, 1 and 2. For an understanding of Williams's, Bloody Tenent, ed. Caldwell, Complete Writings, III, 186-88.

[21]Barrowe, Briefe Discoverie, ed. Carlson, Writings, 1587-90, III, 325.

[22]Robinson, Justification of Separation, ed. Ashton, Works of John Robinson, II, 14 and 16-24; Browne, Reformation without Tarying, ed. Peel and Carlson, Writings, I, 156 and 168; Morgan, Visible Saints, 2, 4, 26, and 55; and Davies, Worship and Theology, II, 59 and 325.

[23]Browne, Reformation without Tarying, ed. Peel and Carlson, Writings, I, 168-70.

[24]Williams, Blovdy Tenent, ed. Caldwell, Complete Writings, III, 101.

[25]Ibid., 184.

[26]Robinson, Of Religious Communion, ed. Ashton, Works of John Robinson, II, 124. See also Browne, Reformation without Tarying, ed. Peel and Carlson, Writings, 169.

[27]See Robinson, Just and Necessarie Apologie, ed. Ashton, Works, III, 9-10; Smyth, Principles and Inferences, ed. Whitley, Works, I, 258-9; and Alan Richardson, A Dictionary of Christian Theology (Philadelphia, 1969), 173-74.

[28]Barrowe, Briefe Discoverie, ed. Carlson, Writings, 1587-90, III, 626.

[29]Williams, Cottons Letter Examined, ed. Guild, Complete Writings, I, 96-97. See also Miller, Orthodoxy in Massachusetts, 99.

[30]Davies, Worship and Theology, I, 44; Morgan, 16; and Powicke, Robert Browne, 87.

[31]Williams, Cottons Letter Examined, ed. Guild, Complete Writings, I, 37. Likewise, Bradford commented that the churches in Massachusetts do under the name secession the same thing that separatists did in old England under separation. See William Bradford, "A dialogue or the sume of a Conference between som younge men borne in New England and Sundery Ancient men that came out of holland and hold England Ann dom 1648," Young, Chronicles of the Pilgrims, 417.

[32]Ibid., 91 and 38.

[33]Barrowe,, Excerpt from Barrow's Conference with Several Clergymen (March 29/30, 1593)," The Writings of John Greenwood and John Barrow 1591-1593, ed. Leland H. Carlson (London, 1970), 236.

[34]Robinson, A Justification of Separation, ed. Ashton, Works, II, 8.

[35]Williams, Cottons Letter Examined, ed. Guild, Complete Writings, I, 91.

[36]Ibid. See also Miller, Orthodoxy in Massachusetts, 96.

[37]See Miller, Orthodoxy in Massachusetts, 67; Morgan, Visible Saints, 28-30; and William Haller, The Rise of Puritanism, Or, the Way to the New Jerusalem as set forth in Pulpit and Press from Thomas Cartwright to John Lilburne and John Milton, 1570-1643 (New York, 1938), 176.

[38]Williams, Cottons Letter Examined, ed. Guild, Complete Writings, I, 108.

[39]Cf. Miller, Orthodoxy in Massachusetts, 69 and 85; Morgan, Visible Saints, 20 and 32; Watts, 29-32; White, 56-57; John A. Goodwin, The Pilgrim Republic (Boston, 1888), 1 and 11; Frederick A. Noble, The Pilgrims (Boston, 1927), 3; and Dewey D. Wallace, The Pilgrims (Wilmington, North Carolina, 1977), 18-19.

[40]Browne, Reformation without Tarying, ed. Peel and Carlson, Writings, I, 164.

[41]Barrowe, "Appendix XVIII: Henrie Barrowe Towchinge the Civill Magistrate," ed. Carlson, Writings of Greenwood and Barrow, VI, 264-65. Furthermore, Robinson commented in 1614, "If the king be a church officer, then he is . . . to be called to his office and so deposed from it, by the church." Robinson, A Justification of Separation, ed. Ashton, Works, II, 278-79.

[42]Barrowe, Briefe Discoverie, ed. Carlson, Writings, 1587-90, III, 644-45.

[43]Ibid., 604.

[44]See, for example, Browne, Reformation without Tarying, ed. Peel and Carlson, Writings, I, 152, 157, 164, and 166.

[45]Henry M. Dexter, The Congregationalism of the Last Three Hundred Years, As Seen in Its Literature (New York, 1880), 101 (hereafter Congregationalism of Three Hundred Years).

[46]Barrowe, Briefe Discoverie, ed. Carlson, Writings, 1587-90, III, 562-63.

[47]See Haller, 182; Watts, 2; and Davies, Worship of English Puritans, 78.

[48]Robinson, A Justification of Separation, ed. Ashton, Works, II, 40.

[49]Browne, Reformation without Tarying, ed. Peel and Carlson, Writings, I, 155-56.

[50]Robinson, A Just and Necessarie Apologie, ed. Ashton, Works, III, 17.

[51]From the point of view of the authorities in separatists appeared to be destroying the status quo, whereas the separatists believed they were merely calling for restitution of the system that Christ first instituted.

CHAPTER II
THE LIFE OF WILLIAMS TO 1652

Though the exact date of Roger Williams's birth is unknown, most likely he was born in London in 1603, the same year James I became king. Williams's father, James, was a London tailor who, though not wealthy, was comfortably situated; his mother's family was part of the landed gentry. Roger was raised on Cow Lane in Smithfield, a suburb of London. There is a dearth of information on the young Williams's childhood, so little is known about the development of his ideas as a youngster. Ola Winslow claims that a variety of nonconformists lived near Smithfield, although there is little evidence to indicate that Williams had either knowledge of or contact with them. Winslow cites two examples of governmental persecution, maintaining it significant that in 1611 two lay preachers--Bartholomew Legate and Edward Wightman--were burned to death in the area near Williams's home, but she is unable to demonstrate any direct connection between the young Williams and either of them.[1]

We do know that Williams received the best education available. In 1623 Williams was able to enter Pembroke College, Cambridge due to the financial patronage of the famous jurist, Sir Edward Coke.[2] Williams's status was that of a pensioner, that is, a person able to pay for his tuition, room, and board. When young Williams matriculated at Cambridge University, James I was still king; James died two years later. While Williams was at the university, in part because of the transition to a new ruler, the conflict between the nonconformists and the crown intensified.

In January 1627 Williams received an A.B. degree, having sworn allegiance to James' favorite three articles, acknowledging the scriptural authority of the Thirty-Nine Articles, the supremacy of the monarch in ecclesiastical as well as civil concerns, and the legitimacy of using the Book of Common Prayer.[3] So in all probability, at that time, Williams was a puritan, not a separatist. In the fall of 1628 Williams left Cambridge without completing the requirements for a M.A. degree. Some historians have speculated that soon thereafter Williams was swayed to the idea of separation. Williston Walker has asserted that, like most early separatists, "here [at the university] he adopted Separatist views."[4] However, there is little evidence to indicate that he actually converted to separatism while at the university.

In the spring of 1629 Williams accepted a position in Essex as chaplain to the puritan household of Sir William Masham, possibly to avoid taking an Anglican pulpit. There he fell in love with a cousin of Masham's wife, but was rebuffed by the woman's mother, Lady Joan Barrington. In response, Williams wrote the mother an extremely untactful letter indicating God's displeasure with her.[5] As to Williams's theological views, he declared in an earlier letter to Lady Barrington that he had refused both a "New England call" and "2 severall livings offerred" to him prior to acceptance of the chaplaincy, indicating his unhappiness with the uniformity of the Anglican system and possibly also his conversion to separatism.[6] During a trip in Lincolnshire in 1629 with John Cotton and Thomas Hooker (1586-1647), both of whom emigrated to Massachusetts in 1633, Williams "presented his Arguments from Scripture, why he durst not joyn with them in their use of Common prayer."[7] This implies that by then Williams had strong separatist tendencies; however, whether Roger was at that moment an avowed separatist is debatable. Soon thereafter Williams indicated that he found it difficult to keep his "soul undefiled in this point [possibly a veiled reference to separatism], and not to act with a doubting conscience."[8]

In 1629 Williams married Mary Barnard, and on 1 December 1630 they sailed from Bristol, England on the ship "Lyon," arriving in Boston sixty-six days later on 5 February 1631.[9] Williams was still young, probably twenty-seven years of age--much younger than the other ministers in New England at that time. His wife was twenty-one. Initially, his arrival was welcomed by the leaders of Massachusetts Bay. In a journal entry, recorded on the day that Williams arrived, Governor John Winthrop of Massachusetts called the young preacher "a godly minister."[10] Not much later Winthrop and others in Massachusetts would have misgivings about him. Within a short time after his arrival, Williams was indeed a self-proclaimed "troubler of Israel" (i.e., of God's chosen people). This epithet became his rallying cry, for in The Bloudy Tenent he wrote that the sons of peace "have borne and still must beare the blurs of troublers of Israel, and turners of the World upside downe."[11]

When asked to become the teacher of the Boston church, Williams refused, later stating that his religious scruples would not allow him to accept the offer. Williams was invited to fill the vacancy because the local pastor, John Wilson, was planning a trip to England. However, Williams declined the call, and even refused to join that congregation as well, on the grounds that the congregation was "an unseparated people" who had not yet repented publicly for having associated with the Church of England. Williams's views are best expressed in his own words written many years later: "Being unanimously chosen teacher at Boston (before your dear father came, divers years), I conscientiously refused, and withdrew to Plymouth, because I durst not officiate to an unseparated people, as, upon examination and conference, I found them to be."[12] Winthrop later wrote that Williams had declared that "the magistrates might not punish the breach of the Sabbath, nor any other offence, as it was a breach of the first table [of the decalogue]."[13]

Unknown to the Bay area Congregationalists, Williams had become an out-and-out separatist who rejected the widely accepted concept of unity of church and state.[14] To the consternation of the establishment in Massachusetts, he insisted on absolute separation from the Church of England and on a whole body of ideas that seemed outrageous and naive to most New Englanders. In one sense, that the people of God disassociate themselves from the Church of England was a demand heard with increasing frequency in the colonies. Yet it was the stress that Williams placed on public renunciation of the Anglican church as antichristian that was completely unacceptable to Massachusetts's authorities. Winthrop and the other leaders were unwilling to repent for having previously associated with the mother church. Williams's inflexible, insensitive response startled and offended the New Englanders who were previously unaware that Williams advocated such an extreme position. The authorities were surprised when Williams suddenly asked them to renounce the official English church and to espouse an uncompromising, separatist understanding of church-state relations. Massachusetts's churches should, Williams insisted, reject communion with the English church while visiting England, and members of the churches in Massachusetts should not even listen to Anglican sermons. Williams went so far as to condemn the Bostonians because they maintained contact and communion with the mother church.

Subsequently, Winthrop and Williams both gave the same account for Williams's refusal to accept the Boston appointment. Winthrop noted in his journal that Williams had "murmured" that the members had not made "a public declaration of their repentance for having communion [previously] with the churches of England."[15] Thus, Williams later wrote that "I durst not officiate to an unseparated people, as upon examination and conference, I found them to be."[16] By the time of his arrival in the colonies, Williams had adopted an inflexible separatist posture in which he demanded that the churches in the New World sever all contact with the corrupt Church of England. Although Williams subsequently highlighted the need for civil liberty, theologically he remained throughout his life a convinced, intolerant predestinarian. Yet, because there is virtually no information available regarding his theological views prior to his arrival in America, it is somewhat unclear how or when Williams developed such a radical posture.

The observations of historian James Ernst notwithstanding, Williams did not reject the clerical position "because the Bay colony denied full liberty of conscience and held to a union of church and state."[17] Rather he refused the appointment because the churches in Massachusetts were not, from his ecclesiastically intolerant perspective, completely pure. His beliefs did not fully mature until the next decade.

In April 1631 Williams accepted a ministerial position in Salem where he assumed the church would be more to his liking because of its separatist inclinations. The principal pastor, Francis Higginson, had died the previous August, and Samuel Skelton, the teacher, was aging. Whether Skelton was a semi-separatist who disavowed total separation as most scholars have asserted, or was (as Philip Gura claims) more extreme in his views than

Higginson and thus clearly a separatist, is uncertain.[18] However, smarting from Williams's criticism and protesting that it had not been consulted, a few days later the General Court of Massachusetts (which exercised legislative, executive, and judicial power) decided to put pressure on Salem to reconsider its offer to Williams. In a letter to Governor John Endecott of Salem, the Court declared that other churches in the colony "looked askance at the Salem Church . . . [for selecting Williams] without advising with the council."[19] Heeding the warning, Salem withdrew its invitation. Compelled to move, Williams and his wife journeyed southward to Plymouth Plantation, where they stayed for nearly two years. While living in the separatist-leaning colony of New Plymouth, Williams served as an unofficial assistant to Ralph Smith, the first pastor to arrive in the New England colonies. While there Williams also developed a close relationship with the Narragansett Indians. Governor William Bradford subsequently called him "a godly and zealous man, with many rare abilities" and wrote that he "prophesied" in a manner that was "well approoved" by the congregation.[20] However, one and one-half years later Bradford said he feared that Williams had begun to "fall into some strang opinions, and from opinion to practise; which caused some controversie betweene ye church & him, and in ye end some discontente on his parte, by occasion wherof he left them some thing abruptly. . . ."[21] Likewise, remembering his experiences in the Netherlands with the erratic Smyth, William Brewster (one of the leaders of the Pilgrim fathers) feared Williams had succumbed to fanaticism--that he "would run the same course of rigid Separation and anabaptistry which Mr. John Smyth, the se-baptist at Amsterdam, had done." Though originally he had thought that the church in Plymouth was open to "seek the Lord further," Williams ultimately realized that Plymouth was not wholeheartedly separatist, and after a sojourn of two years he left, probably by request.[22]

Though both Salem and Plymouth were settled by separatists, the somewhat moderate views of the leaders in those two colonies differed from Williams's inflexible position. While Plymouth had declared its separation from the Church of England, for Williams the proclamation was not absolute enough. He wrote that when the settlers in Plymouth traveled to England they attended Anglican services and thus were not truly separated. Because

Bradford, Brewster, and the other Pilgrims were unwilling to accept Williams's idea of complete separation, they were unwilling to welcome the extreme views of Williams and prevailed on him to leave. So we see that Williams's rigidity affected his relationship with the churches in Plymouth and Salem as well as the one in Boston.

Another reason Williams was viewed as a pariah in Plymouth was what Winthrop called a "dangerous" treatise in which Williams contended that the Plymouth patent issued by King James was invalid and should be returned.[23] Williams's contention was that the patent did not give the English title to the land of the Indians. A decade after the banishment, Cotton wrote that Williams was expelled in part because of his "violent and tumultuous carriage against the Patent."[24] However, Williams's treatise on the patent was but one aspect of a substantive, doctrinal dispute with Massachusetts. Williams was not expelled merely because he opposed the king's decree expropriating the land of the native Americans, though his disagreement on that specific issue triggered a comprehensive inquiry by the General Court.

In the summer of 1633 Williams returned to Salem to assist (in an unofficial capacity) the ailing Skelton. On 2 August 1634 Skelton died, and in the summer of 1635 the Salem congregation invited Williams, to the chagrin of the authorities in Boston, to become their pastor. Angry that he had not been consulted, Winthrop remarked that Salem "had chosen Mr. Williams their teacher, while he stood under question of authority, and so offered contempt to the magistrates."[25] Yet in the ensuing months Williams proceeded "to seek after the Lord Jesus without halting."[26] On 4 September 1633 John Cotton arrived in Boston, soon thereafter to take the ministerial post Williams had rejected.

Williams's experience in Plymouth had not taught him caution, and he was again involved in controversy soon after his arrival in Salem. The eighteenth-century Baptist historian, Isaac Backus, declared that Williams officially was invited back to Salem but gives no source to justify that claim.[27] Whereas Plymouth was a separate colony, Salem was not; it was part of Massachusetts Bay. Hence, once again Williams threatened the Boston establishment. For the next year and one-half Williams found himself constantly differing with the colonial leadership. A rigid separatist since 1631, he was preaching against those principles fundamental to the New England tradition of non-separating congregationalism. Williams later wrote that under his leadership (if not before) "the Church of Salem was known to profes separation."[28]

In April 1634 the General Court enacted a law requiring all adult males who were not freemen to take an oath of loyalty to the Court in order to ensure the political allegiance of the citizenry in event of a conflict with the crown. Williams refused to take the oath and spoke out against the ordinance.[29] "[He] had taught publicly, that a magistrate ought not to tender an oath to an unregenerate man." In the next chapter, Williams reasons for that view will be explained. The same year Williams and Skelton criticized the other clergy in Massachusetts for holding a series of biweekly meetings, "fearing it might grow in time to a presbytery or superintendency, to the prejudice of the churches' liberties."[30] Indeed, an advisory synod was held two years later at Newton. Convinced that the churches of England were unchristian, Williams accused the holy commonwealth of Massachusetts of having erected erroneously state churches. Finally, on 16 August 1635, he addressed a letter "to his own church [in Salem], to persuade them to renounce communion with all the churches in the bay, as full of antichristian pollution, etc."[31] When the congregation refused to do so, Williams withdrew from the Salem church.

After having tried often to persuade Williams to renounce his public pronouncements in favor of separatism, in the summer of 1635 the General Court opted to charge Williams with the "dangerous opinions" associated with separatism. According to Winthrop, on 8 July Williams's was indicted by the General Court on four counts

> for divers dangerous opinions, viz. 1, that the magistrate ought not to punish the breach of the first table...; 2, that he ought not to tender an oath to an unregenerate man; 3, that a man ought not to pray with such, though wife, child, etc.; 4, that a man ought not to give thanks after the sacrament nor after meat, etc....The said opinions were adjudged by all, magistrates and ministers,...to be erroneous, and very dangerous, and the calling of him to office, at that time, was judged a great contempt of authority.[32]

In early October of that same year, Williams went on trial before the General Court for teaching dangerous opinions with "all the ministers in the bay being desired to be present."[33]   The clergy tried without avail to convince Williams's of his errors. "Mr. Hooker [the pastor of New Town (Cambridge)] was appointed to dispute with him, but could not reduce him from any of his errors."[34] Unconvinced, Williams steadfastly refused to be intimidated and to renounce his fundamental belief in the principle of absolute separation. As a result, after one day of dispute, a decree was issued expelling him forever from the colony for having "broached & dyvulged dyvers newe and dangerous opinions, against the aucthoritie of magistrates, as also writt lres of defamacon, both of the magistrates & churches here."[35] Thus, in October 1635 Williams was banished from the Bay, a decree which remained in effect for more than two hundred years. William was sentenced to leave the territory within six weeks, but because he fell ill, the authorities in Boston issued a respite until spring, provided that he cease "to draw others to his opinions."[36] William Bradford said he later told Williams that he was "as good as banished from Plymouth as from Massachusetts" in 1636 as well.[32]

In January 1636 the General Court learned that about twenty people who were sympathetic to Williams's plight were meeting in his home. Governor John Haynes and his assistants decided to "send him into England by a ship then ready to depart."[38] Warned soon thereafter by Winthrop of the impending deportation, Williams was forced to flee in the dead of winter into the wilderness with Thomas Angell, a servant. During that time he later wrote that he was "sorely tossed for one fourteen weeks, in a bitter winter season, not knowing what bread or bed did mean."[39] Through the snow, Williams made his way to an Indian settlement near the Seekonk River where he was befriended by the Indians and later met four associates from Salem. With the help of the Narragansett Indians, Williams and his party built a shelter on the east side of the river and waited for spring to come. But Governor Winslow sent a messenger who told them to proceed to the other side of the river because they were within the jurisdiction of Plymouth. So, in the early spring of 1636, Williams and his companions crossed the

Seekonk River; they are said to have landed at Slate Rock where they built a town on a site purchased from the Indians and founded the settlement of Providence. Five years earlier Williams had crossed the wide Atlantic, bringing with him a whole series of controversial religious beliefs that caused a stir among all the leaders in Massachusetts and eventually led to his expatriation.

Rhode Island was based on the innovative principles of separation of church and state and liberty of conscience for all. From the beginning, no one in Providence Plantations was forced to attend any church. Derogatorily called "Rogue Island," Williams's colony became a refuge for outcasts. Many dissenters found religious freedom in Providence and on nearby Aquidneck Island, purchased by Williams from the Indians for Anne Hutchinson and her party. Few barriers were established to keep undesirable people out. Jews, Quakers, and other outcasts were allowed to settle without suffering recrimination. Anne Hutchinson, William Coddington, Samuel Gorton, and many other dissenters settled in Rhode Island within a span of a few years.

The story of the baptists in America begins with Roger Williams. Most likely Williams was a Calvinistic, not an Armenian, baptist. According to Governor Winthrop, "Mr. Williams rebaptized himself and some ten more" in March of 1639, marking the establishment of the Baptist Church of Providence, the first baptist church in America.[40] Katherine Scott, Anne Hutchinson's sister, converted Williams to believers' baptism. However, he was not a baptist for very long. Having decided that such a baptism was not authentic, Williams withdrew from all institutional churches, including the church he had founded in Providence. Williams never again attended any church on a regular basis. For the rest of his life he remained skeptical of organized religion. He had moved from condemnation of state churches to skepticism about all formal churches.[41] While Williams never again joined another formally organized church, he upheld for the remaining forty-three years of his life the baptist and separatist principles that he cherished dearly.

Some scholars have speculated that soon thereafter Williams became a member of the English sect known as the seekers, a mystical group that rejected all churches and ministries. The seekers contended that no true church would exist on earth until God sent a new group of apostles; in the meantime they worshipped the Lord through an inward, spiritual search. The contention is that Williams, like John Smyth many years before, followed an ideological progression from puritanism to separatism to the radical baptist position, but unlike Smyth, Williams became a seeker. Contact with the seekers then moved Williams a step closer to his final intellectual destination--religious toleration.

The extent to which Williams was in contact with the English seekers, even though he remained an antipaedobaptist as before, is uncertain. Although Richard Baxter (1615-1691) and Robert Baillie (1599-1662) both mention the seekers and Williams's association with them, in his writings Williams refers to himself as seeking but never mentions that he is a member of the seekers. Indeed, Williams never said he was a member of any church or group after 1640.[42] Thus, Williams's relationship with the seekers is uncertain. He never called himself a seeker, but did accentuate the need for believers to search for truth. If Williams was a seeker, he was of the Calvinistic variety who condemned inordinate spiritualization. "He was definitely not," as William Lee Miller has written, "a seeker in the way that a twentieth-century person would use the word."[43]

In August 1637 Providence was incorporated as a town and a preliminary government established. Yet Williams waited until the spring of 1643, at the age of forty and seven years after his banishment, before travelling to far-off England to obtain a charter from Parliament for his new colony. Williams disembarked in England in the midst of the turmoil of a civil war in which questions of church and state were of paramount importance, and soon entered the thick of the dialogue with several works concerned with religious liberty and the relationship between Christianity and culture. Indeed, Williams arrived at a crucial moment during the era of the Long Parliament. A few days prior to his landing, the Westminster Assembly held its first meeting. While in London he met John Milton, Sir Henry Vane, John Canne, and other nonconformists.

Because Parliament was preoccupied with the civil war and because emissaries from Massachusetts sought to block his efforts, Williams had to wait for nearly one year before obtaining the Narragansett Patent on 14 March 1644. On 17 September Williams disembarked again at Boston with the charter in hand. The General Court of Massachusetts allowed him to travel safely across their territory with the understanding that permission for passage would not be granted in the future to him. The general assembly of Providence elected Williams as its chief officer of its new colonial government a few weeks later, although the exact date is unknown since no record of the meeting is extant.

While Roger Williams was a prolific writer, it was not until his return to England in 1643 that he put his ideas concerning separation and liberty into writing. Except for George Fox Digg'd out of his Burrowes (1676), all of Williams's books were printed during two extended visits to England: the first in 1643-44, the second in 1651-54. The trips provided him with an opportunity to have his views published. In July 1644, about three months after Williams obtained the patent for Providence and left England, his famous plea for religious tolerance and liberty, entitled The Bloudy Tenent of Persecution, was published in London. That controversial tract immediately distinguished him as an eloquent and powerful voice in search of tolerance and liberty in a society built on principles of unity and loyalty. In 1652 he penned The Bloody Tenent Yet More Bloody in which he argued that Jews, Catholics, Moslems, and Armenians should be given unqualified religious freedom.

Chapter 2

Endnotes

[1]Williams's early life is mentioned in Samuel H. Brockunier, <u>The Irrespressible Democrat, Roger Williams</u> (New York, 1940), 4-9; and in Ola Elizabeth Winslow, <u>Master Roger Williams: A Biography</u> (New York, 1957), 3 and 7-23. For further information on Legate and Wightman, see Leonard W. Levy, <u>Treason Against God: A History of the Offense of Blasphemy</u> (New York, 1981), 183-90.

[2]Chief Justice under James I, Coke is best known as a proponent of the preeminence of the tradition of the common law as the ancient, pre-Norman law of the land.

[3]Winslow, 70.

[4]Williston Walker, <u>A History of the Congregational Churches in the United States</u> (New York, 1894), Vol. III: The American Church History Series, 129.
[5]Roger Williams, "Letter to Lady Barrington," <u>New England Historical and Genealogical Register</u> (1889), XLIII, 319.

[6]Ibid., 317.

[7]Roger Williams, <u>The Bloody Tenent Yet More Bloody: By Mr. Cottons endevour to Wash it white in the Blood of the LAMBE; . . .</u> (London, 1652), ed. Samuel L. Caldwell, <u>Complete Writings</u>, III, 65.

[8]Williams, <u>Cottons Letter Examined</u>, ed. Guild, <u>Complete Writings</u>, I, 88.

[9]See the 5 February 1631 entry in Winthrop's journal. John Winthrop, <u>Winthrop's Journal</u>, ed. James K. Hosmer (New York, 1908), I, 57. Most of the information for Williams's life in New England is in his own writings or in Winthrop's journal.

[10]Winthrop, <u>Journal</u>, ed. Hosmer, I, 47.

[11]Williams, <u>The Bloudy Tenent</u>, ed. Caldwell, <u>Complete Writings</u>, III, 58.

[12]This explanation of Williams's refusal to accept the teaching position is found in a letter he wrote to John Cotton's son in 1671, thirty-five years after the expulsion. That Williams was offered the appointment, which Cotton later accepted, rests primarily on his testimony in a private letter and secondarily on a statement by Winthrop in his journal. Williams, "Letter to John Cotton, Jr.," ed. Bartlett, <u>Complete Writings</u>, VI, 356; Winthrop, <u>Journal</u>, ed. Hosmer, I, 62.

[13]Winthrop, <u>Journal</u>, ed., Hosmer, I, 62.

[14]See Winthrop, Journal, I, 322; and Hubbard, A General History, 204.

[15]12 April 1631 entry in Winthrop's Journal. Winthrop, Journal, ed. Hosmer, I, 62.

[16]Williams, "Letter to John Cotton, Jr.," ed. Bartlett, Complete Writings, VI, 356. Cf. Winthrop, Journal, ed. Hosmer, I, 61-62.

[17]James E. Ernst, Roger Williams, New England Firebrand (New York, 1932), 432-33.

[18]Hubbard, A General History, 181; and Gura, 36. See also Brockunier, 46; and Gilpin, 26, 35, and 38.

[19]Winthrop, Journal, ed. Hosmer, I, 62.

[20]Bradford, History of Plymouth Plantation, ed. Ford, II, 161.

[21]Ibid., II, 161.

[22]For Brewster's remarks, see Nathaniel Morton, New England's Memoriall (Cambridge, Massachusetts, 1669), 78. The "seek the Lord further" quote is in Williams, "Letter to John Winthrop, Sr. from New Plymouth [1636 or 37]," ed. Bartlett, Complete Writings, VI, 3.

[23]Winthrop, Journal, ed. Hosmer, I, 116; and Allyn B. Forbes, ed., Winthrop Papers (Boston, 1929-47), III, 147.

[24]John Cotton, The Blovdy Tenent of Persecution, Washed and Made White in the Bloud of the Lambe (London, 1647), 28. As mentioned in the introduction, Cotton also told Williams that he was expelled "for ought I know, for your corrupt Doctrines, which tend to the disturbance both of civil and holy peace." Cotton, A Letter of Mr. John Cottons, ed. Guild, Complete Writings, I, 334.

[25]Winthrop, Journal, ed. Hosmer, I, 155. Winthrop is the source for the date Skelton died; see Winthrop, Journal, ed. Hosmer, I, 130.

[26]Roger Williams, Cottons Letter Examined, ed. Guild, Complete Writings, I, III.

[27]Isaac Backus, A History of New England with Particular Reference to the Denomination of Christians Called Baptists (Boston, 1777), I, 56.

[28]Williams, Cottons Letter Examined, ed. Guild, Complete Writings, I, 378.

[29] Entry for 30 April 1634 in Winthrop's Journal, ed. Hosmer, I, 149. See also Shurtleff, ed., Massachusetts Bay Records, I, 115; and Williams, Cottons Letter Examined, ed. Guild, Complete Writings, I, 325.

[30]November, 1633 entry to Winthrop's Journal. Winthrop, Journal, Hosmer, I, 112-13.

[31]Winthrop, Journal, ed. Hosmer, I, 162.

[32]Entry for 7-8 October 1635 in Winthrop, Journal, ed. Hosmer, I, 162.

[33]Ibid., I, 163.

[34]Shurtlett, ed., Massachusetts Bay Records, I, 160.

[35] Winthrop, Journal, ed. Hosmer, I, 168.

[36]Winthrop, Journal, ed., Hosmer, I, 154. Cf. Williams, Cottons Letter Examined, ed. Guild, Complete Writings,, 41.

[37]In 1936--three hundred years after the expulsion--the edict banishing Williams was rescinded.

[38]January 1636 entry in Winthrop's Journal. Winthrop, Journal, ed. Hosmer, I, 168. Haynes was elected governor in May 1635 defeating both Winthrop and Thomas Dudley.

[39]The quote is from an epistle that Williams wrote more than three decades after his banishment. Roger Williams, "Letter to Major Mason (June 22, 1670)," ed. Bartlett, Complete Writings, VI, 335-36

[40]Winthrop, Journal, ed. Hosmer, I, 297. Whether Williams or Clarke was the first baptist in America is debatable. Most scholars have contended Williams's rebaptism receded all others; LeRoy Moore and Thomas Bicknell, however, have claimed that Clarke's baptism took precedence. LeRoy Moore, Journal of Church and State 7 (Spring, 1965), 181-89; and Thomas W. Bicknell, The Story of John Clarke (Providence, 1915), passim.

[41]Regarding Williams's withdrawal from the Baptist Church of Providence, Winthrop records: "Mr. Williams and many of his company [in Providence], a few months since, were in all haste rebaptized . . . and now he was come to question his second baptism." Winthrop, Journal, I, 309.

[42]The primary source indicating an association between Williams and the seekers is a passage written by Robert Baillie, Professor of Divinity at Glasgow University, who served as a Scottish delegate to the Westminster Assembly. Baillie wrote in a letter written in 1644 that Williams had influenced many seekers: "Sundrie of the Independent partie are stepped out of the Church, and follows my good acquaintance Mr. Roger Williams; who sayes, there is no church, no sacraments, no pastors, no church-officers, or ordinance in the world, nor has been since a few years after the Apostles," Robert Baillie, "Letter for Mr. D[ickson]," The Letters and Journals of Robert Baillie A.M.: Principal of the University of Glasgow, ed. David Laing (Edinburgh, 1841-42), II, 212. The seekers will be discussed in chapter V.

[43]William Lee Miller, The First Liberty: Religion and the American Republic (New York, 1986), 202. Miller continues: "For Parrington and others to call him a 'seeker,' after he has, at the end of his life, for his reasons, left the ministry and all churches, may lead to a considerable mistake. . . .Williams was a 'seeker' only after the proper institutional expression, in the wilderness of the world, of the truth he had already found."

CHAPTER III

WILLIAMS'S RADICAL POLITY AND POLITICS[1]

During the course of his first sojourn in England, Williams issued five tracts, the last three anonymously. The first, A Key into the Language of America , was published in London in September 1643, having been written at sea on the crossing from America. Gregory Dexter, who later followed Williams to Providence, was probably the printer.[2] A Key served several purposes and can be interpreted on various levels. Firstly, it was a vocabulary and phrase book of the language of the Narragansett Indians. Secondly, it was a practical guide for dealing with Indians and a sociological analysis of their mores and life. Thirdly, it was a didactic commentary on the nature of civilization and of what it means to be Christian. Through a series of personal reflections, including various sections on "Spirituall Observations," A Key conveyed to the English-speaking world the message of tolerance. By redefining such terms as "civilitie" and "Christianitie," Williams indirectly attacked both the distinction between pagan and European customs and the conviction that England was a chosen nation. Because the tone was not openly contentious, most readers probably were unaware of this more subtle, third level of interpretation.[3]

Williams did not write his first pamphlet against Cotton and the Congregational establishment in Massachusetts until the 1640s, and it was in response to a letter written eight years before by Cotton. In late 1643 A Letter of Mr. John Cottons to Mr. Williams, penned in 1636 but previously unpublished, was printed in London by an unknown source. Its purpose was to demonstrate "that those ought to be received into the Church who are Godly, though they doe not see, nor expressly bewaile all the pollutions in

Church-fellowship, Ministry, Worship, Government."[4] While the discourse was concerned primarily with church organization, Cotton opened the dispatch with the comment that Williams had banished himself by refusing to have communion with the Massachusetts congregations.[5] That statement provided Williams with an opportunity for the first time to discuss his expulsion publicly. On 5 February 1644, the memory of banishment still clear, Williams composed a rejoinder under the title Mr. Cottons Letter Lately Printed, Examined and Ansvvered. Williams focused initially on the issue of qualifications for church membership, but instead of discussing exclusively theological issues, Williams used Cotton's opening comment as a justification for discussing the events surrounding his exile as well.[6] He contended that Christ's witnesses or martyrs should lead the reformation, referring to two witnesses mentioned in Rev. 11: 3-12 who testified to the Lamb of God at the time of the second advent. Four days later Williams challenged Cottons' allies in the Westminster Assembly, the five Dissenting Brethren or Independents, with a brief plea for liberty of conscience dedicated to the presbyterian-controlled Parliament, Qveries of Highest Consideration. Qveries was a polemical attack on the non-separating position expressed in the Assembly by the conservative Independents. It argued vehemently against government intervention in religious affairs.[7]

In July of 1644, at a critical moment during the English civil wars, Williams anonymously issued his principal work and his first comprehensive statement in favor of religious liberty: The Bloudy Tenent, of Persecution, for cause of Conscience.[8] As the title indicates, Williams viewed persecution for cause of conscience as a bloody doctrine. The Bloudy Tenent presents Williams's mature thought regarding religious toleration. A bold, uncompromising statement in favor of liberty, it was Williams's major contribution to the controversy of the times. One month later The Bloudy Tenent was ordered burned in London by Parliament.[9] Addressed to Parliament, The Bloudy Tenent is a four hundred and twenty-one page commentary on three works: (1) A Most Humble Supplication of Many of the King's Majesty's Loyal Subjects (1620), an appeal for freedom of conscience written in milk (i.e., according to Williams, in blood) by an English baptist incarcerated in Newgate prison. (2) Cotton's letter in 1635 in response to that baptist plea; and (3) A Model Of Church and Civil Power which was the first written explanation by the clergy in Massachusetts regarding church polity and church-state relations.

Most likely, A Most Humble Supplication was composed in London by a member of Thomas Helwys's baptist congregation. Michael Watts and others have contended that John Murton (d.1626), who was imprisoned roughly from 1613 through 1620, was the author.[10] Murton was a baptist precursor of the tolerationist position later championed by Williams. Williams praised A Most Humble Supplication in The Bloudy Tenent.

An ecclesiastical plan presented by a group of Massachusetts clergy to the people in Salem soon after Williams's ouster, A Model of Church and Civil Power was the first attempt to formulate the New England Way and thus to defend the view that the magistrate has a right to intervene in church affairs. (Later the same ideas were codified in the Cambridge Platform in 1648.) Developed in response to the need for "one uniforme order of dissipline [sic] in the churches," the Model presented the Massachusetts position of non-separating congregationalism based on the view that Massachusetts was the New Israel.[11] The document sought to justify the right of magistrates to interfere in religious affairs in order to stamp out schism and heresy. In reply to the Model Williams declared that Christ never asked secular rulers to help him in church affairs. Although Williams attributed the document to Cotton, most likely a group of clergy in Massachusetts penned it concurrently.

In 1645 (after departing for America), Williams's second brief work about conversion of the Indians, Christenings make not Christians, was printed in England.[12] In it Williams maintained that the term "heathen" refers to all men not in the church, not only to Indians and that the time for conversion of the Indians had not yet come. Williams denied that aspect of the royal charter for the Massachusetts company which declared that "the propagation of the Gospel is the thing we do profess above all to be our aim in settling this Plantation," thereby challenging an essential aspect of the attempt to build a "city on a hill," as Winthrop called it.[13]

In 1647, a few weeks before the Cambridge Synod, Cotton wrote two replies to Williams's works: A Reply to Mr Williams his Examination, justifying Williams's banishment, and The Bloudy Tenent Washed White in the Bloode of the Lambe, refuting The Bloudy Tenent, of Persecution and defending persecution of those who sin against their own conscience.

In 1651 Williams travelled again to England because his charter for the colony of Providence had been effectively nullified by William Coddington's appointment as governor of the colony of Rhode Island. Williams and Clarke went to obtain a new document from the Rump Parliament. During this second journey Williams composed five works and developed a friendship with John Milton. In March 1652 at the age of forty-nine, Williams published The Fourth Paper presented by Major Butler to counteract the Independents' proposals before Parliament for magisterial involvement in religious affairs.[14] The sectarian William Butler,(a soldier in Cromwell's army) had argued, as Williams did, for absolute freedom of conscience.

One month later four more works were printed: (1) The Hireling Ministry none of Christs was an appeal to Parliament to reconsider compulsory financial support for the clergy. Williams maintained that "a hireling ministry"--one supported financially by the state--is anathema and to be rejected.[15] (2) The Bloody Tenent Yet More Bloody: By Mr. Cottons endevour to wash it white in the Blood of the Lambe was Williams's longest treatise and most important work of the 1650s. His objective was to demonstrate again, as he had done in the first Tenent , that the doctrine of political persecution for cause of conscience is "one of the most Seditious, Destructive, Blasphemous and Bludiest in any or in all the Nations of the World."[16] In Yet More Bloody Williams discussed both the nature of state-enforced persecution and the necessity of placing limits on the spiritual authority of civil leaders. Cotton died before writing a rejoinder. (3) Later the same year Williams penned a letter to his wife Mary on the nature and way of the spiritual life which was published under the title Experiments of Spiritual Life and Health.[17] The "experiments" to which he referred were spiritual or devotional experiences. Williams's ecclesiology is reflected in several of his comments. For instance, he explained that it is healthy to long "after the enjoyment of God, and of Christ, in a visible, and open profession of his own holy worship and Ordinances, separate from all false worships,

Gods, and Christs."[18]   (4) Published in the same year, The Examiner Defended was Williams's most temperate attack on magisterial intervention in religious affairs and essentially condenses the views of The Bloudy Tenent written eight years before.[19] It was a reply to the views contained in The Examiner Examined which had declared that the English monarch should function as a nursing father, as the king in ancient Israel had. In 1654 he returned home to Providence.

Williams contended that no one could be certain of truth. While he was convinced that God would show the light in the last days, he believed that in the meantime any claim to know truth lacked absolute finality. In the Bloudy Tenent he called truths "inventions" of men. Consequently, within his thought, ambiguities abound and ideas often are convoluted. W. K. Jordan has observed that the "thought [of Williams] must be regarded as unsystematic, eccentric, undisciplined, and occasionally tedious." Indeed, in The Examiner Defended Williams admitted the difficulty of determining Absolute Truth, "And Oh how many are the Skreens, the Veils, the Hoods, . . .and Colours, by which the lustre and shining of that which we call Truth, is hidden and eclipsed from us!" And in The Bloudy Tenent, while discussing the nature of the true church, Williams talks of his uncertainty: "I yet cannot see it proved that light is risen, I mean the light of the first institution, in practice."   Notwithstanding, Williams's most important beliefs are discernible. In particular, his theory of church-state relations and of religious liberty are unequivocal.[20]

Neither Williams's ecclesiology nor his political theory were thoroughly developed, since his writings were generally controversial pieces, often autobiographical in nature. Nonetheless, his view of civil and spiritual power is lucid. Williams distinguished clearly between nature and grace. His was a doctrine of two completely distinct kingdoms: one of the world, the other of Christ. There is "a true difference between the church and the world, and the spiritual and civil state."[21] Williams declared that in the past the functions of God and Caesar had been confused. He spoke for all sectarians when he wrote that a fusion between them, whether on the basis of a state church or otherwise, is impugned by scripture and by the blood of the martyrs. He ridiculed that "commonly received and not questioned opinion, viz., that the civil state and the spiritual, the church and the commonwealth, they are like Hippocrates's twins, they are born together, grow up together, laugh together, weep together, sicken and die together." Astutely Williams observed that an amalgamation of the political and religious spheres is inherently problematic; "[it] is a mingling and confounding of heaven and earth together."[22] He urged an absolute institutional as well as a functional separation. For the seventeenth century it was a revolutionary plea.

Though himself ordained, Williams was seldom an ally of the influential men of the cloth. He taught that ministers were not the only ones able to convey spiritual truths. Moreover, after fleeing from Massachusetts in the winter of 1636, Williams sought to escape from the formalism of religion. He opposed excessive ministerial as well as magisterial power: Christian arrogance toward non-believers; the demarcation between clergy and laity; and the clergy's reliance on temporal power to convey the Gospel message. Williams asserted that sly, arrogant clerics have misled political leaders into interfering in ecclesiastical affairs in order to gain money and power for themselves. Such self-centered officials have erroneously adhered to Mosaic law rather than Christ's proclamation of grace and eternal life for the elect. Williams believed that the official clergy were often antichristian, idolatrous, arrogant, and intolerant.

There are degrees of separateness. Tudor separatism was not nearly so pervasive, logical, or absolute as Williams's version. Williams conjectured that church and commonwealth are organically different in origin, aim, nature, authority, function, competence, principles, and prerogatives. Ideally, the relation between the spiritual and the natural is one of distinctiveness, not association. "So unsuitable is the comingling and intangling of the civil with the spiritual charges and government that the Lord Jesus and his apostles kept themselves to one."[23] Each institution exercises its potential when independent of the other. Both have suffered irreparable damage from an unnatural, unscriptural association. Only when independent of the political state is the church able to maintain its individual identity.

Whereas the early separatists attached a negative connotation to the term "separation," for Williams it meant something constructive. As Ralph Barton Perry has pointed out, Williams's depiction of the nature and purpose of both church and state was positive.[24] Each realm has its own distinct sphere and method of enforcement, its own rules and rulers. He adhered rigidly and literally to Christ's remark to "render to Caesar that which is Caesar's," writing: "But as the civil Magistrate hath his charge of the bodies and goods of the subject: So have the spiritual Officers, Governors and overseers of Christs City or Kingdome, the charge of their souls, and soul safety."[25] The office of magistrate was established by the Lord to preserve the civil peace; that of minister to convey grace. God had instituted a division of powers with the advent of Christ. As Paul declared in Romans 136, "the powers that be are ordained of God." The lord is master of both the secular and religious world. By nature both social and religious, man exists simultaneously in two unrelated, divinely-sanctioned societies. To be precise, however, at times Williams delineated three, not two, spheres: the natural, the civil, and the spiritual. He seldom mentioned the natural order, and when he did, he often spoke of the civil as its subset. "[A] state or land is none else but a part of the world, and if so . . .it is but natural, and so lieth as the whole world doth in wickedness."[26]

For Williams the provinces of church and of commonwealth are strictly limited.   Though possessing prerogatives, each also confronts constraints. Since the advent of Christ, the ecclesia has authority over people's spiritual lives, but has no right to intervene in the civil realm; the government is concerned solely with social behavior, yet lacks authority over human souls or consciences.

> The power of the civil magistrate is superior to the church policy in place, honor, dignity, earthly power in the world; and the church superior to him, being a member of the church, ecclesiastically; so that all the power the magistrate hath over the church is temporal, not spiritual, and all the power the church hath over the magistrate is spiritual, not temporal.[27]

Williams adhered to a doctrine of two tables. Civil authorities may enforce the second table of the law (i.e., the last six commandments of the Decalogue) concerned with external behavior and social relations among people, but not the first table (i.e., the first four commandments) regarding the human conscience. The individual and church have sole responsibility for matters relating to the first table. A person should not, therefore, be imprisoned or banished by the state for his religious convictions. "Will the Lord Jesus," Williams asked rhetorically in The Bloudy Tenent, ". . .joyne to His Breastplate of Righteousnesse, the breastplate of iron and steele?"[28] Obviously the answer for Williams was "no." Christ refused to rule through use of the power of the sword. "The civil state was never," he wrote in 1644, "invested by Christ with the power and title of Defender of the Faith."[29] Only when free, will the church prevail over heresy and impiety. Although Williams believed that state officials did serve God, he rejected the Calvinist notion that they were ministers of Christ. He makes a subtle distinction between the involvement of God and of Christ in secular affairs, contending that Christ would not reign over the world until the advent of the millennium.

In a 1654 letter to the people of Providence, Williams used a ship as a metaphor to demonstrate the precise determinants of the jurisdiction of each sphere.[30] Christ had designated his ministers to be the unchallenged masters of the ship which is the Church. The prince is merely one of a number of passengers on that ship with no special jurisdiction. As pilot, the minister alone determines the ship's course. On the other hand, the magistrate is in charge of another vessel, the ship of State and he is to be judged by his leadership skills, not by his convictions. To be a Christian does not make a monarch a better ruler. The moral of the analogy of the two ships is that insofar as they behave in accord with he law, passengers have the right to worship as they please. Christians, including the clergy, are simply passengers (citizens); their rights and authority are no greater than those of hypocrites and unbelievers. They are unable to justify, on the basis of spirituality, interference in secular affairs.

Unlike Williams, Cotton contended that the best magistrates are church members, since only members of the body of Christ have sanctifying grace. In a letter penned a few months after Williams's banishment, Cotton affirmed that in the commonwealth of Massachusetts the responsibility of the church is to prepare "fit instruments both to rule and to choose rulers." As the story of the ship indicates, Williams disagreed vehemently with Cotton's views, declaring that there is no such thing as a "Christian captain, Christian merchant, physician, lawyer, pilot, father, master, and (so consequently) magistrate."[31]

The battle for congregational autonomy having already been won by his predecessors, it was unnecessary for Williams to dwell on ecclesiastical concerns. As a controversialist, he focused instead on such pressing and disputable issues as separation and religious liberty. Nevertheless, Williams commonly spoke of Christ's heavenly society as a "garden" or paradise in which the predestined elect live apart from the world.[32] This analogy points out the sharp distinction that he made between the holy kingdom of God and the impure world. This differentiation accounts for Williams's radicalism. For example, Williams opposed the use of the medieval term "Christendome;"[33] he was convinced that there was no such thing as a Christian commonwealth. To call a nation Christian was a contradiction in terms, since all nations were composed primarily of the reprobate who were by definition not Christian. His demand for purity of worship allowed the unregenerate no opportunity to be treated in the same manner as the saints. Further, the author of The Bloudy Tenent disapproved of Massachusetts's oath of loyalty, viewing such pledges as religious acts. He was adamant that the faithful should not worship with the unconverted. His was a parochialized ecclesiology.

Williams's view of the nature of the church and ministry is less clear than Cotton's or his predecessors'. Hence, it is difficult in any particular passage to determine whether he is referring to the church as a universal, spiritual entity or as a concrete, historical reality. Some historians have asserted that Williams ignored the existence of a visible ecclesia. According to William Warren Sweet, "Williams stressed the inner experience, and to him the true church was an invisible entity made up of the regenerate--an inward experience without physical form. The visible church, therefore, to Williams was of slight importance."[34] Although Sweet's comments are an oversimplification, there is a grain of truth in his observation; Williams was uncomfortable with all existing hierarchical organizations and fixed forms of worship. Indeed, he was unable to believe in any existing ecclesia. As a seeker of truth, he was disenchanted with all known views of the church. For him, further light was needed before he could be certain. That is to say, in due time Williams insisted on the purely spiritual nature of the church and believed that no true church would exist on earth until Christ's return.[35]

Yet, paradoxically, throughout the greater part of his life, Williams continued to write about the visible church and to attend public worship services. Williams's writings are filled with references to the empirical church. As a separatist, he was preoccupied with questions of personal holiness and institutional purity. The overall tone of Williams's writings highlights particular visible churches, even though they are remote form the world, a "garden in the wilderness."[36] Several examples may be cited. Whenever Williams mentions the suffering of a church he usually is referring to a specific, persecuted nonconforming congregation. The Bloody Tenent Yet More Bloody refers to the institutional church "as the spiritual officers and governors of the church bear not in vain the spiritual and two-edged sword coming out of the mouth of Christ."[37] Also Williams disputed Cotton by retorting:

> Although the Discusser [Williams] cannot to his Souls satisfaction conclude any of the various and severall sorts of Churches extant to be those pure golden Candlesticks framed after the first pattern, Rev. 1:12-20. Yet doth he acknowledge golden Candlesticks of Christ Jesus extant; those golden Olive trees and candlesticks, his Martyrs or Witnesses, standing before the Lord . . . .[38]

He declared that those who oppose the "visible kingdome, and the visible Christ Jesus in point of his kingdome, church and worship" were hypocrites.[39] Williams believed that because of its congregational polity, the apostolic church was the visible model for all other Christian bodies. As a separatist, Williams espoused the view that "the Church of Christ is a congregation of Saints."[40] He accepted the notion of a very early apostasy and declared that since Constantine's day no true church has been extant.[41] By 1642 he had become disillusioned with the urgent search for holiness on earth. Presumably uncertain about church order, he declared the effort futile until the dawn of a new age. In a debate with two prominent Quakers in 1673, thirty years after publication of The Bloudy Tenent, Williams condemned his opponents for overly spiritualizing the scriptures and the church.[42]

In the words of Williams: "A civill Government is an Ordinance of God, to conserve the civill peace of people, so farre as concernes their Bodies and Goods."[43] Williams's contention was that state officials should not interfere in church affairs because religion is so important that it can truly exist only to the extent to which people are free. Ironically, however, the net result of his definition of Christ's heavenly society has been the opposite; such a limited and definitive understanding has tended to minimize religions's role and impact within society. In his two discourses on the bloody tenet, Williams viewed the church as merely one among many voluntary associations within the larger, secular society. As such, its authority and rights are no greater than any other private corporation. For Williams the church was no longer the primary institution within society. He envisioned a more limited role for the ecclesia; its authority no longer extends all over the world to all aspects of society. The church is no longer the ultimate authority on earth, as it was during medieval times. In The Bloudy Tenent Williams wrote:

> The church or company of worshippers (whether true or false) is like unto a Body or Colledge of Physitians in a Citie; like unto a Corporation, Society or Company of East Indie or Turkie Merchants, or any other societie or company in London . . . because the essence or being of the Citie is essentially distinct from those particular Societies. The Citie was before them, and stands absolute and intire, when such a Corporation or Societie is taken down.[44]

Such a view particularizes the church and secularizes the state. It rejects the organic concept of an established or state-imposed Christianity, limiting divine authority to supremacy over a few congregations not over society in general. The church was, for Williams, no longer the medium for activity of the Lord in the world. Inherent within Williams's definition of the church is the assumption that the body of Christ is no longer the all-embracing dominant social institution that it had been since the time of the Emperor Constantine. Williams rejected what had been for centuries the normative understanding of Christianity: the notion of a universal church on earth. His stress on particular churches was probably a major reason for his disavowal of the doctrine of the Church Universal. With a strictly limited understanding of the church, Williams articulated and institutionalized what had been for the early separatists a spontaneous, personal reaction against the injustice of a specific tyrannical system. Whereas his English mentors had maintained simply that they had a right to exist and should be permitted to worship alongside the official system, Williams taught that a particular church of saints was the only institution worthy of the name. His was an atomistic understanding.[45]

Unlike his forerunners who resisted only the calcified orthodoxy of the English system, again and again, Williams militated against all state churches, including Massachusetts's city on a hill. The concept of an established church, even though congregational, was per se anathema. The moment the Christian religion received state support it ceased to be "a true church." "The national church . . a state church, whether explicit as in Old England, or implicit as in New, is not the Institution of the Lord Jesus Christ." In Cottons Letter Printed, Examined Williams contended that national churches "are false and to be separated from," because they confused the spiritual and political spheres. Such an unholy alliance contradicts the essence of the Christian faith. Opposition to established churches was a natural outgrowth of Williams's convictions.[46]

Williams believed that the post-Reformation principle of cuius regio, eius religio ("whose is the government, his is the religion") was among the greatest of evils. Attacking the application of that rule during the previous century, Williams queried:

> Who knowes not how easie it is to turne, and turne, and turne againe whole Nations from one Religion to another? Who knowes not that within the compasse of one poore span of 12 yeares revolution [1547-1559], all England hath become from halfe Papist, halfe Protestant, to be absolute Protestant; from absolute Protestants to absolute Papists, from absolute Papists to absolute Protestants?[47]

Williams was convinced that the many changes from Catholicism to Protestantism occurred in part because the English crown was allowed to employ the sword to crush its ecclesiastical enemies. "True it is, the Sword may make. . .that only works the All-powerfull God, by the sword of the Spirit in the hand of his Spirituall officers."[48] For Williams the implication is that it is foolish to assume that the truth of a religion depends on the whims of a monarch, indeed of any earthly person or thing. He pointed out that if the magistrates "have fundamentally and originally, as men, a power to governe the Church, to see her doe her duty, to correct her. . . . [This is] to pull God and Christ, and Spirit out of Heaven, and subject them unto naturall, sinfull, inconstant men, and so consequently to Sathan himselfe."[49] When politicians have the power to determine a people's faith the consequences are hypocrisy and social instability. Anglican England could have avoided all the confusion if the distinction between God and Caesar had remained clear.

As Williams pointed out, Cotton and other ministers in Massachusetts relied primarily on proof-texts from the Old Testament to justify an established church, notwithstanding sanctions also found in Romans 13:1 and elsewhere.[50]

> Mr. Cotton retreats into the land of Israel, and calls up Moses and his Laws against Idolaters, Blasphemers, Seducers, &c. [sic] When he is challenged for producing the Pattern of a National Church when he stands only for a Congregationall . . . Mr. Cotton retreats to Moral Equity, that the Seducer and he that kills a Soul should die.[51]

Like many in England who over the centuries had viewed their nation as elect, the authorities in Massachusetts perceived themselves as having been specially chosen, believing that God had made a covenant with them. For them, the Reformation having failed in the motherland, New England was the new Israel. But that covenant was conditional on their adherence to the true Christian faith and thus implied that it was necessary for the state to enforce the true religion. Naturally the leaders in Massachusetts were infuriated when Williams condemned magisterial involvement.

Williams contended that the fusion in ancient Israel of religion and politics was a unique occurrence. For only during that brief moment in history was it the duty of the magistrate to protect the faith and his right to wield the sword to enforce conformity.[52] That was because the Israel of the Old Testament had been chosen to participate in a special covenant with Yahweh. However, after the crucifixion "the Lord cast them [the Jewish people] out of his sight, destroyed that nation church, and established the Christian church."[53] Moreover, Jewish theocracy came to an end, and a new dispensation of "particular and congregational churches all the world over" began.[54]

> The Lord Jesus hath broken downe the Wall of Division between the Jewes and the rest of the Nations of the World, and sent forth his Ministers (Wisedomes Maidens) unto all Nations, to bring in (by the Gospels Invitation) Proselites, Converts, Disciples, such as should Eternally be saved, to begin that heavenly and Eternall Commupion in Heaven, here in an holy and visible Worship on Earth.[55]

Boldly, Williams rejected the notion of Massachusetts as a New Israel in favor of a doctrine of a spiritual Canaan. He held that there is a radical difference between the Old and New Testaments, and he interpreted ancient Israel allegorically, not literally. Because Jesus did not use coercion, never again would there be a holy commonwealth like that experienced by Moses and his flock. Williams asserted that no modern nation is Israel's successor. No group has a special covenantal relationship with the Lord, nor an accompanying right to use the power of the law to coerce consciences. "The pattern of the national church of Israel was a none-such, unimitatable by any civil state in all or any of the nations of the world beside."[56] "The spiritual Israel . . . is the only antitype of the former figurative and typical."[57] Cotton and his clerical colleagues, he felt, are mistaken to seek to emulate the pattern of Israel. Neither England nor Massachusetts could claim election as the basis for an alliance of church and state, since neither was chosen.[58] Nor could they legitimately, as Cotton sought to do through his Moses his Judicialls, enforce the Mosaic law as the Jews had. Only the Lord's church can force compliance with religious principles. "Let Master Cotton now produce any such national in the whole world whom God in the New Testament hath literally and miraculously brought forth of Egypt, or from one land into another, to the truth and purity of his worship," Williams beseeched the authorities in Massachusetts.[59] Williams wrote: "What Land, what Country now is Israels Parallel and Antitype, but that holy mysticall Nation the Church of God? . . . .Gods people are now in the Gospel brought into a spirituall land of Canaan."[60] Christ instituted two distinct, governmental spheres to replace the previously unified system.

Vehemently, Williams opposed erection of a holy commonwealth, viewing the patterns of Geneva, London, and Boston as antichristian apostasies. Like the continental anabaptists, Williams held that the incorrect notion of the corpus christianum or Christendom had begun with Constantine. In the fourth century the Constantinian ideal of a Christian commonwealth had wrongfully usurped the position of the true Christian faith. "Christianity fell asleep in Constantine's bosom."[61]

> The poor servants of Christ, for some hundereth of years after the departure of the Lord enjoyed no other power, no other Sword nor Shield but spirituall, until it pleased the Lord to try his children with Liberty and ease under Constantine (a soarer Tryall then befell them in 300 years persecution) under which temporall protection, munificence and bounty of Constantine, together with his temporall Sword, the Church of Christ soon had too much honey or worldly ease, authority, profit, pleasure, & c.[62]

In A Reply to Mr. Williams Cotton asserted that the New England Way was the closest system to what would exist "if the Lord Jesus were here himselfe in person."[63] Such a view makes little allowance for tolerance. Even Williams acknowledged that the New England way of non-separating congregationalism was closer to the Christian ideal than Anglicanism was, yet he nevertheless condemned Cotton and the leaders in Massachusetts for implicitly having instituted another national church and for condoning compulsion in religion. He said that the baptists are the closest to Christ's ideal.[64]

> I affirm (what ever are the pretences, pleas and coverings to the contrary) that that Church estate, that religion and worship w[hich] is commanded or permitted to be but one in a country, nation or province (as was the Jews religion in that typical land of Canaan) that Church is not in the nature of the particular Churches of Christ, but in the nature of a Nation or state Church.[65]

Nor did Massachusetts avoid the problem by limiting membership to visible saints, since its antichristian alliance of church and state violated the Lord's mandate.[66]

> By compelling all within their Jurisdiction to an outward conformity of the Church Worship, of the Word and Prayer, and maintenance of the Ministry thereof, they evidently declare that they still lodge and dwell in the confused mixtures of the uncleane and cleane, of the flock of Christ, and Herds of the World together, I meane in spirituall and religious worship.[67]

By using "the sword of steel" to enforce religious uniformity, Williams asserted, Massachusetts's establishment committed "soul-rape," since "to force the Consciences of the Unwilling is a Soul-rape."[68] "By compelling all within their jurisdiction to an outward conformity of the church worship," Williams added, "they evidently declare that they still lodge and dwell in the confused mixtures of the unclean and clean."[69] Indeed, Williams stated that the Bay's theocratic system was contrary to the normal pattern throughout the world, since some non-Christian nations even practice religious liberty.

The political thought of Roger Williams differed little from those of presbyterians or congregationalists, except in his insistence on rights and liberties based on the principle of separation of church and state. Williams was unique in considering the state as an exclusively secular institution; its purpose was to insure social order. By demonstrating that the power of the state was limited, he defined clearly magisterial authority.

Since Williams considered politics within the province of man rather than of God, he preferred no set form of government; the governed should be free to determine the specific type of political system. The secular arm was ordained by God, but the best form was left for men to determine based on the circumstances. The form could change as the need arose. Williams would probably have accepted any government--monarchical or democratic-- if it afforded its people soul liberty and allowed the spirit of God to operate (although he seems not to have thought well of kings).[70]

Regarding the issue of the right to rebel against the state, Williams was relatively conservative. Indeed, as Edmund Morgan indicates, except in the matter of church-state relations, Williams's general attitude was socially "conventional and static."[71]   For example, in Williams's 1652 tract The Examiner Defended, the ship analogy stresses that within each realm the ruler is to be obeyed.   Williams highlighted the need for all passengers, regardless of personal opinions, to defer to the captain's authority.   In his words:

> Now in a Ship there is the whole, and there is each private Cabbin.   Hence, not to study, and not to endeavour the common good, and to exempt our selves form the sense of common evil, is a treacherous Baseness, a selfish Monopoly, a kinde of Tyranny, and tendeth to the destruction both of Cabin and Ship, that is, of private and publike safety.[72]

So we see that Williams's social ethic was essentially conservative, not revolutionary, except in the realm of church-state relations. He believed that the power of a magistrate or a minister is absolute within his respective domain.[73] "Notwithstanding this liberty," said Williams, "the commander of this ship ought to command the ship's course, yea, and also command that justice, peace and sobriety, be kept and practiced, both among the seamen and all the passengers."[74]

Williams refused to condone rebellion against a political leader because he was unjust or not a Christian. The faithful were to obey anyway. The magistrate's religious beliefs made no difference. Rather what was important was whether the ruler performed his civil duties properly. A Christian should obey the magistrate, even though he be "pagan or popish" and should pray for his well-being.[75]

Williams sought to enhance magisterial authority in secular affairs that order might be preserved. Like Cotton and Winthrop, by contending that the fifth commandment applied to civil as well as to familial superiors, Williams highlighted respect for civil and religious authority. Moreover, he felt that the poor, i.e., those without property, should neither be allowed to vote or rule. In Providence laws were made by majority vote of males who as heads of households were given the franchise.[76] And, in spite of the fact that Williams believed that each man is part of a community and subject to civil law without regard to religion or creed, he did not intend that his call for liberty lead to license. He stated, "That ever I should speak or write a title that tends to. . .an infinite liberty of conscience, is a mistake, and which I have ever disclaimed and abhorred"[77].

Chapter 3

Endnotes

[1]Secondary works that are helpful in understanding Williams's teachings are Mauro Calamandrei, "Neglected Aspects of Roger Williams' Thought," Church History (September, 1952), Vol. II, No. 3, 239-58; Henry Chupack, Roger Williams (New York, 1969); John Garrett, Roger Williams: Witness Beyond Christendoom (New York, 1970); W. Clark Gilpin, The Millenarian Piety of Roge Williams (Chicago, 1979); W. K. Jordan, The Development of Religious Toleration in England (London, 1936), III, 472-506; Perry Miller, "Roger Williams: An Essay in Interpretation," The Complete Writings of Roger Williams, VII, 5-25; and Edmund S. Morgan, Roger Williams: The Church and the State (New York, 1967).

[2]Roger Williams, A Key into the Language of America: or, An help to the Language of the Natives in that part of America, called New-England (London, 1643), ed. James H. Trumbull, Complete Writings, I, 77-284. Williams had most of his publications printed clandestinely, as the early separatists often did.

[3]I would surmise that there were at least three reasons Williams's approach was uncharacteristically subtle: the nature of the work, he was listed as the author, and a desire to be diplomatic.

[4]John Cotton, A Letter of Mr. John Cottons to Mr. Williams (London, 1643).

[5]John Cotton, A Letter of Mr. John Cottons Teacher of the Church in Boston, in Nevv-England, to Mr. Williams a Preacher there (London, 1643), ed. Guild, Complete Writings, I, 295-312.

[6]Williams, Cottons Letter Examined, ed. Guild, Complete Writings, I, 313-396.

[7]Roger Williams, Qveries of Highest Consideration, Proposed to Mr. Tho. Goodwin, et. al. (London, 1644), ed. Reuben A. Guild, Complete Writings, II, 251-275.

[8]Williams, The Bloudy Tenent, ed. Caldwell, Complete Writings, III, 3-425. The Bloudy Tenent is divided into two parts. The first section, composed of eighty-one chapters, is a line-by-line reply to Cotton's answer to the plea from the Newgate prisoner and an appeal for religious liberty. The second part, consisting of fifty-seven chapters, affirms the indispensability of complete separation and rebuts the theological justification in Massachusetts' ministerial document, A Model of Church and Civil Power.

[9]According to the records of Parliament for 9 August 1644, it was "ordered that Mr. White do give order for the publick burning of one Williams his booke, intitled, & c. the tolerating of all sorts of religion." Commons Journal (15 March 1642 to 24 December 1644), III, 585.

[10]Michael R. Watts, The Dissenters: From the Reformation to the French Revolution (Oxford, 1978), 49-50. The theme of the baptist's letter was "Whether Persecution for cause of Conscience be not against the Doctrine of Jesus Christ the King of Kings." See Cotton, Bloody Tenent Washed, I, 2.

[11]Shurtleff, ed., Massachusetts Bay Records, I, 142.

[12]Roger Williams, Christenings make not Christians, Or A Briefe Discourse concerning that name Heathen, commonly given to the Indians, also concerning that great point of their Conversion (London, 1645), ed. Perry Miller, Complete Writings, VII, 29-113.

[13]The charter is printed both in Shurtleff, ed., Massachusetts Bay Records, I, 3-20; and in Francis N. Thorpe, ed., The Federal and State Constitutions, colonial charters, and other organic laws of the States, territories, and Colonies, now or heretofore forming the United States of America (Washington, 1929), III, 1846-60. The Winthrop quote is found in John Winthrop, "A Modell of Christian Charity," in Perry Miller and Thomas H. Johnson, eds., The Puritans: A Sourcebook of Their Writings (New York, 1963) revised edition, I, 197 and 199.

[14]Roger Williams, The Fourth Paper presented by Major Butler, To the Honourable Committee of Parliament, for the Propagating the Gospel of Christ Jesus (London, 1652), ed. Perry Miller, Complete Writings, VII, 119-141.

[15]Roger Williams, The Hireling Ministry, ed. Miller, Complete Writings, VII, 146-191.

[16]Williams, Bloody Tenent Yet More Bloody, ed. Caldwell, Complete Writings, IV, 3-529.

[17]Roger Williams, Experiments of Spiritual Life & Health, And their Preservatives which the weakest Child of God may get assurance of his Spirituall Life and Blessednesse (London, 1652), ed. Miller, Complete Writings, VII, 45-113.

[18]Ibid., 82.

[19]Roger Williams, The Examiner Defended, In A Fair and Sober Answer to The Two and twenty Questions which lately examined the Author of Zeal Examined (London, 1652), ed. Miller, Complete Writings, VII, 195-279.

[20]Jordan, III, 474-75; Williams, Examiner Defended, ed. Miller, Complete Writings, VII, 198; and Williams, Bloudy Tenent, ed. Caldwell, Complete Writings, III, 65.

[21]Ibid., 94.

[22]Ibid.; Williams, Yet More Bloody, ed. Caldwell, Complete Writings, IV, 81-83; and Williams, Bloudy Tenent, ed. Caldwell, Complete Writings, III, 4, 94, and 127.

[23]Williams, Bloudy Tenent, ed. Caldwell, Complete Writings, III, 94.

[24]Perry, Puritanism and Democracy, 349-50.

[25]Williams, Bloudy Tenent, ed. Caldwell, Complete Writings, III, 127. See also p. 36.

[26]Ibid., 180.

[27]Williams, The Bloudy Tenent, ed. Caldwell, Complete Writings, III, 76.

[28]Ibid., III, 151 and 227.

[29]Ibid., III, 120. For John Cotton's view justifying use of "the civil sword," see Cotton, The Bloudy Tenent Washed, 66-68.

[30]Roger Williams, "Letter to the Town of Providence (January, 1654-55)," ed. John R. Bartlett, Complete Writings, VI, 278-79.

[31]Ibid., 81.

[32]Williams, Bloudy Tenent, ed. Caldwell, Complete Writings, III, 94, 184, and 233.

[33]Ibid., 184 and 320.

[34]Sweet, Religion in Colonial America, 126.

[35]Williams, Bloudy Tenent, ed. Caldwell, Complete Writings, III, 56.

[36]Ibid., III, 94, 184, and 233.

[37]Williams, Yet More Bloody, ed. Caldwell, Complete Writings, IV, 292.

[38]Ibid., 383.

[39]Ibid.

[40]Ibid., 143.

[41]Williams, Bloudy Tenent, ed. Caldwell, Complete Writings, II, 64, 174, and 178.

[42]Roger Williams, George Fox Digg'd out of his Burrowes, or an Offer of Disputation, . . . (Boston, 1676), ed. J. Lewis Diman, Complete Writings, V, 44 and 95.

[43]Ibid., 249.

[44]Ibid., III, 73. Eight years later Williams declared that "the church is one society in the city, as well as the society of Merchants, Drapers, & c. And if it be civil justice to protect one, then the other also." Williams, Yet More Bloody, ed. Caldwell, Complete Writings, *IV*, 80.

[45]Williams described the church as "the Citie of God," "a Colledge of Physitians," "the Citie of the Lord," "the Christian Commonweale," "a company of beleevers," "like a school," and "God's mystical Israel." Williams, Bloudy Tenent, ed. Caldwell, Complete Writings, III, 246, 275, 281, 284, 286, and 306; and Williams, Cottons Letter Examined, ed. Guild, Complete Writings, I, 64.

[46]Williams, Bloudy Tenent, ed. Caldwell, Complete Writings, III, 66 and 367; and Williams, Cottons Letter Examined, ed. Guild, Complete Writings, I, 91.

[47]Williams, Bloudy Tenent, ed. Caldwell, Complete Writings, III, 325. See also Williams, Qveries of Highest Consideration, ed. Guild, Complete Writings, II, 260.

[48]Williams, Bloudy Tenent, ed. Caldwell, Complete Writings, III, 136.

[49]Ibid., 250.

[50]Ibid., 68.

[51]Williams, Yet More Bloody, ed. Caldwell, Complete Writings, IV, 42-43.

[52]Williams, Cottons Letter Examined, ed. Guild, Complete Writings, I, 77-78; and Williams, Bloudy Tenent, ed. Caldwell, Complete Writings, III, 239 and 281.

[53]Williams, Yet More Bloody, ed. Caldwell, Complete Writings, IV, 131. See Williams, Bloudy Tenent, ed. Caldwell, Complete Writings, III, 239.

[54]Williams, Bloudy Tenent, ed. Caldwell, Complete Writings, III, 66. See also Williams, Cottons Letter Examined, ed. Guild, Complete Writings, I, 63.

[55]Williams, Hireling Ministry, ed. Miller, Complete Writings, VII, 157.

[56]Williams, Yet More Bloody, ed. Caldwell, Complete Writings, IV, 29.

[57]Williams, Bloudy Tenent, ed. Caldwell, Complete Writings, III, 351 and 322. See also pp. 317 and 351.

[58]Ibid., 254; and Williams, Yet More Bloody, ed. Caldwell, Complete Writings, IV, 181.

[59]Williams, Yet More Bloody, ed. Caldwell, Complete Writings, IV, 181.

[60]Williams, Bloudy Tenent, ed. Caldwell, Complete Writings, III, 322 and 303.

[61]Ibid., 184. See also pages 67, 174, and 178.

[62]Williams, Yet More Bloody, ed. Caldwell, Complete Writings, IV, 384.

[63]Cotton, A Reply to Mr. Williams, 237.

[64]Williams, Cottons Letter Examined, ed. Guild, Complete Writings, I, 42-44; Williams, Bloudy Tenent, ed. Caldwell, Complete Writings, III, 200; and Williams, "[Letter] For Mr. John Winthrop, [Dec. 10, 16149]," ed. Bartlett, Complete Writings, VI, 188.

[65]Williams, Yet More Bloody, ed. Caldwell, Complete Writings, IV, 389.

[66]Williams, Cottons Letter Examined, ed. Guild, Complete Writings, 91; and Williams, Bloudy Tenent, ed. Caldwell, Complete Writings, III, 15-17; and Miller, 153.

[67]Williams, Bloudy Tenent, ed. Caldwell, Complete Writings, III, 234.

[68]Williams, Examiner Defended, ed. miller, Complete Writings, VII, 268. Cf. Williams, Bloudy Tenent, ed. Caldwell, Complete Writings, III, 124-25.

[69]Williams, Bloudy Tenent, ed. Caldwell, Complete Writings, III, 64.

[70]Williams, Bloudy Tenent, ed. Caldwell, Complete Writings, III, 343 and 180. See Robert D. Brunkow, "Love and Order in Roger Williams's Writings," Rhode Island History Vol. 35 (November, 1976), 18.

[71]Morgan, Roger Williams, 25. See also Joseph Dorfman, The Economic Mind in American Civilization, 1606-1865 (New York, 1946), I, 69.

[72]Williams, Examiner Defended, ed. Miller, Complete Writings, VII, 203.

[73]Williams, Bloudy Tenent, ed. Caldwell, Complete Writings, III, 228.

[74]Williams, "Letter to the Town of Providence (Jan., 1654-55)," ed. Bartlett, Complete Writings, VI, 379.

[75]Williams, Bloudy Tenent, ed. Caldwell, Complete Writings, III, 236. See also p. 197.

[76]Brunkow, 20-22.

[77]Williams, Letter to Major Mason," ed. Bartlett, Complete Writings, VI, 334.

CHAPTER IV

SEPARATIST ANTECEDENTS

Separatism emerged in England during the reign of Elizabeth I when in 1580 or 1581 Robert Browne organized in Norwich, the nation's second largest city, the first overtly congregational church.[1] He was the first Englishman to break publicly with the Elizabethan church and to propagate openly the separatist world view, at the age of thirty having established a congregation which was clearly independent of the national church. Although Browne may not have been the only puritan to entertain congregational notions, he was the first to do so publicly. Hence, he deserves to be called the first prominent separatist in England. He was aided by his college friend, Robert Harrison (d.1585).

In A Treatise of Reformation Without Tarying for Anie, published in Middleburg during his exile, Browne pleaded in 1582 for abandonment of the Church of England and establishment of independent churches, while simultaneously declaring his loyalty to the regnum. Yet, complete separation of church and state was never his intent, nor was he initially interested in instituting congregationalism. In the beginning, Browne neither advocated nor established a new ecclesiastical system. At first his ecclesiology was based on specific criticisms rather than on extensive theological reflection. Separation was a strategy by which to achieve reform rather than an end in itself. Initially, Browne still hoped for a reformation from within. His reason for gathering a group of true believers in Norwich was neither to espouse a novel polity nor to justify such an action theologically. Only after leaving the official church was Browne confronted with questions of ecclesiastical theory and practice for which he is known today. Even then he urged a conditional dissociation in which the <u>avant-garde</u> was to separate only temporarily from the larger church, not separation of church and state as Roger Williams later propagated it. Browne never pleaded for two completely separate forms of government: one civil, the other spiritual.

In any case, since the prelacy refused either to purify or to expel the unregenerate, Browne felt he had no other choice but to defy the authorities by seceding. By 1580 the unorthodox decision to separate seemed to him, as it did to Williams more than fifty years later, the only remaining way to achieve thorough reform. Abandoning the established church was a risky and drastic step. But, for Browne, change from within the church began to appear unlikely, as the Elizabethan hierarchy firmly opposed further reform. From his point of view, the inherent nature of "the episcopal beast" was to resist Divine truth. No longer able to tolerate the situation, Browne decided thorough reform could be achieved only by leaving.

Browne believed that he and his followers were God's elect--visible saints--chosen to lead the way toward a complete reformation "without tarying for anie."[2] In so doing, Browne rejected the Calvinist notion that reform would be carried out through state action, contending instead that those who see the need should bring about change, for God would not excuse those who tarried. For Browne the true church was composed of only a few saints, not the citizenry of an entire nation. Like Williams, Browne believed in a strict Calvinist doctrine of election, but did not reject completely the Genevan system of church polity. Whereas Williams drew non-Calvinistic ecclesiological conclusions, Browne did not.

Based on the assumption that forced worship is unscriptural, Browne contended that only the gathered church is true. "The Church planted or gathered, is a companie or number of Christians or beleeuers, which by a willing couenart made with their God, are vnder the government of god and Christ, and kepe his laws in one holie communion."[3] For Browne, as for most seventeenth-century puritans, there was no universal church, only specific congregations. Antithetical to the medieval doctrine of a <u>corpus christianum</u>, such voluntarism became the fundamental principle of congregationalism and the basis for Williams's sophisticated notion that all social organizations, including churches, are voluntary associations, only the state in its civil responsibilities is not.

Autonomy of each local church is fundamental to Brownism. Throughout A Booke Which Sheweth Browne argues for self-governing bodies. Yet, like Cotton and the congregationalists of Massachusetts in the 1630s, Browne did not believe in complete independence for each congregation, but taught that churches should be loosely connected.[4] Fellowship with other bodies of saints was a duty and a privilege. A company unable to determine the will of God should seek advice from other congregations, but as a group, not as individuals. Unlike Williams, Browne was not an isolationist; he defended the use of "synods or meetings of sundry churches" in situations in which "the weaker churches seeke helpe of the stronger."[5] Synods are to be encouraged insofar as they are limited to an advisory capacity, for no church is to have authority over another, nor are synods to have a permanent status. Finally, a synod was to be composed of the churches themselves, not of representatives of each church. Williams, on the other hand, remained skeptical about the propriety of synods.

Browne promulgated neither complete separation of church and state nor absolute religious liberty which later became the hallmarks of Williams's career. He desired freedom of worship primarily for himself and his associates. Unintentionally, Browne pioneered new approaches. His views of the church and of church-state relations were radical for the time.

In Reformation without Tarying, his classic work on church-state relations, Browne wrote, "Let us leave to the Magistrates; to rule the common wealth in all outward iustice, belongeth to them; but let the Church rule in spiritual wise, and not in worldlike maner."[6] Although the magistrates have jurisdiction over secular affairs, their sacerdotal authority is limited: Political rulers have no position in the Church per se, except based on spiritual maturity.[7] "The magistrates . . .haue," wrote Browne, "no Ecclesiastical authoritie at all, but onlie as anie other Christians, if so they be Christians." They are not "spiritual kings."[8] Ultimately Christ is a superior to all worldly authority. Either the prince is a believer and thus subject to the will of God, or he is not and has no position in the Body of Christ.

Browne was the first English cleric to insist that magisterial dominion over the church be limited. Browne wrote that if the demands of the prince are contrary to those of the Lord "we must not give place by yielding unto them, no not for an hour . . . .[The magistrate's demands] must not be rule unto me of this and that duty, but as I see it agree with the word of God." He continued, "Wee must firste looke what is the Lordes will and charge, and then what is the will of man."[9] Likewise, "The Magistrates commaundement must not be a rule vnto me of this and that duetie, but as I see it agree with the worde of God."[10]

Browne said that "the Lords people is of the willing sorte."[11] He believed that ministers, rather than civic officials, should discipline their flocks and enforce the faith. Thus, ecclesiastical reform is the responsibility of religious leaders, not of government officials, for to do otherwise is to give the secular authorities more influence in church affairs than Christ has. Are not those who tarry for a ruler "ashamed thus to slander the Magistrate" by waiting for official government action?[12] "For the spiritual power of Christ and his Church . . .they take from Christ and give to the Magistrate."[13]

As a loyal subject, Browne believed that in the civic arena the queen's jus divinum is the highest on earth. The queen may brandish the sword in temporal concerns. She may even "put to death all that deserve it by law, either of the Church or commonwealth, and none may resist her. . . by force or by wicked speeches."[14] However, she lacks the right to "compell religion, to plant Churches by power, and to force a submission to Ecclesiastical gouernement."[15] To force people to believe is to "usurp the throne of Jesus Christ."[16] The church need not depend on the government's police power.

Browne's position on church and state seems ambiguous, having varied throughout the course of his life. Originally, Browne was willing to accept government-sponsored reform. He had no intention of instituting a permanent separation from the established church. A state church was for him axiomatic. Thus, for a significant part of his adult life, Browne was an erastian congregationalist. During both the pre- and post-separatist phases of his intellectual development, Browne accepted the idea of a state church. Evidently, he never relinquished the desire for national reform. Despite his disillusionment with the halfway reformation of the Elizabethan church, even during his separatist phase Browne had erastian tendencies: For instance, he seems to have believed,without realizing the contradiction, that government officials should enforce the true religion, even though eventually he said that pastors should discipline believers.[17]   When the queen refused to bring about a thorough reform, Browne chose to separate--all the while protesting his loyalty to the crown and insisting on the transient nature of his actions. A national church, at that point, may or may not have seemed acceptable.

While Browne believed that royal authority should be circumscribed and not employed "to compell religion," he also asserted that it could be used as "as a means of keeping the churches under state control and so of ensuring in them a reasonable amount of unity in belief and practice."   "Our magistrates," he continued, "[may] reform the church and command things expedient for the same" just as Moses had reformed the faith of Israel.[18]

Though Browne contemplated an absolute monarchy, his innovative notions abetted the trend toward ecclesial democracy. Browne taught an indwelling Christ. His doctrine of the church was of a spiritual monarchy ruled by Jesus as Lord. He advocated Christocracy, not democracy. But the leader, Jesus, was invisible; hence, Christ's will was not always discernible. Accordingly, democracy tended to emerge within the Brownist communities due to various interpretation of the divine will. Browne was aware that dissension might erupt in light of different understandings, but he was confident that the magistrates would be able to curb it.[19]

In 1593 at the insistence of his relative, Lord Burghley, Browne overtly made peace with the authorities, renounced his aberrations publicly, and spent the last forty years of his life in obscurity. After conforming during the 1590s, Browne accentuated the right of the magistrate to interfere in churchly affairs, arguing that "because the church is in a commonwealth, it is of their [the magistrates'] charge; that is concerning the outward provision and outward justice, they are to look to it."[20]   After 1593, he accepted political intervention in the life of the church. Browne's career and writings are filled with such contradictions. Until the early seventeenth century most separatists were dubbed Brownists by their enemies.

Browne died in 1633--thirteen years after the voyage of the Mayflower and three years after Williams arrived in Massachusetts.[21] Williams never met Browne. By the time Williams arrived at Cambridge University in 1625, Browne's career as a schismatic had long since ended. Yet, at Cambridge, Williams probably read Browne's tracts or heard about him. Williams mentions the Brownists, despite their notoriety, in Cottons Letter Examined.[22]

In the late 1580s soon after Browne returned from a sojourn in Holland, the mantle of puritan radicalism passed from Norwich to London to the leadership of Henry Barrowe and his associate John Greenwood (c.1550-1593). Considered enemies of both state and church, these London subversives flourished from 1587 through 1593 when they were executed for publishing seditious works. The authorities accused them of seeking to overthrow the established church by calling for the abolition of the episcopacy and elimination of royal supremacy over religious affairs. Whereas Browne's career ended with a recanting, Barrowe's came to a close with a hanging. Yet, after Barrowe's death, the group continued to meet under the leadership of Francis Johnson, first in London then in Amsterdam.[23] Though a layman, Barrowe was an effective spokesman for the separatist cause. Through his writings, nonconformity progressed to a new level. Barrowe's ecclesiology and invectives against the church resembled Browne's, yet his arguments were simpler, clearer, and more developed. Barrowe's writings were extensive; his prose made a lasting impression of several generations of English dissenters. Williams probably read Barrowe's writings, while at Cambridge from 1625 to 1627. Williams mentions Barrowe in Cottons Letter Examined,in The Bloudy Tenent, and indirectly in The Bloudy Tenent Yet More Bloudy.[24]

During questioning by Archdeacon Hutchinson, Barrowe defended his belief that the Church of England was false by attacking four aspects of the Anglican faith: the manner of worship, the all-inclusive nature of membership, the false ministry, and the antichristian polity. On the first point Barrowe felt that the English system of worship was completely idolatrous. "The administration and worship of this Church is not according to the Word of God."[25] The way of venerating God was false. Because Anglican worship services employ mechanical prayers given in a superstitious way, the Church of England is popish. Devotion should be based on the

Word of God, not on a book derived from Rome. The Book of Common Prayer was popish and encouraged a ministry which would not pray or preach in their own words. The buildings of the English Church are "Babylonish synagogues," he declared.[26] Barrowe asserted that even to participate in the official religious service was to oppose God, a claim made five decades later by Williams.

Second, Barrowe wrote, "The profane and ungodly people are received [erroneously] into and retained in the bosom and body of their churches." The Church of England allowed the unconverted to belong to parish churches. Barrowe called such Anglican church-goers "the profane multitude."[27] Barrowe's assault on the policy of admitting all citizens to the national church was tantamount to a rejection of the prevailing notion that the visible church included the unregenerate. "The people as they stand are not called orderly to the faith, but stand mingled togeather in confusion."[28] He said that the English Church is "utterly destitute of this power of Christ [to excommunicate] and wholly overruled by the erroneious power of antichrist in his limbes, these bishops and their clergie." Greenwood added that a church is based on "the profession which the people make," not on a geographical area.[29]

Barrowe also condemned "the false and antichristian ministry imposed upon their churches."[30] The Tudor ministry was false, he argued, because it was imposed by force, not based on the apostolic pattern, and because clergy were appointed by bishops, not by congregations. "The ministerie set ouer them is not the true ministerie of the gospell which Christ hath appointed to his Church in his testament." The Barrowist interpretation of the ministerial office was highly subjective. There is no true ministry without a purified church. The holiness of the congregation is a precondition for an authentic ministry.

Finally, he believed that the government of the Church of England was "unlawful and antichristian."[31] The Anglican church was popish, not based on a covenant, and undemocratic, since members of the congregation were uninvolved in the decision-making process. "The ecclesiasticall gouernment, Courts, officers, & Cannons are not," Barrowe added,

"according to the testament of Christ, but new & antichristian." "The false
and antichristian government wherewith their churches are ruled."[32]

Like Browne, Barrowe postulated that the true church is founded on a
covenant. Obedience to God's will was the most important condition of that
pact. Barrowe's opponents said he taught a doctrine of works righteousness,
but he maintained that obedience by the elect to the covenant was a product
of divine grace. The Church of England was false, he said, because it had no
such contractual base.

Barrowe defined the church exclusively, as Browne did, thereby
rejecting John Calvin's moderate understanding.[33] In a 1590 publication
Barrowe defined a true church as one which "conteyneth in it all the Elect of
God that haue bin, are, or shall be. . . . It consisteth of a companie and
fellowship of faithful and holie people gathered in the name of Christ
Jesus."[34] It was a body "ioyned together as members of one bodie; ordered
and gouerned by such officers and lawes as Christ in his last will and
Testament hath therevnto ordeyned." In light of this definition he found the
Church of England "in euerie point transgressing and defectiue."[35]

Barrowe dared to say it was the duty of each Christian to determine
which church is properly constituted and to abandon any church which is not
in accord with the will of God--a very modern notion.

> It behooveth us therefore, . . . to examine our ways, and to
> ponder our estate, whether we be in that broad way that
> leadeth to destruction amongst those multitudes over whom
> the whore sitteth and reigneth or in the straight and narrow
> way which leadeth to everlasting life, with Christ's little flock.[36]

In answer to the question of the authority by which the separatists sought to
reconstitute the church, Barrowe made it clear that their actions were in
accord with scripture. God was clearly calling his people to flee the grip of
the whore of Babylon. The command in the Bible was clear: separate and
reconstruct the church.[37]

While Barrowe's understanding of church government was internally
less democratic than Browne's, he wrote that the local congregation is "one
bodie unto Christ; all the affairs of the church belong to that bodie
together."[38] Appointment to all ecclesiastical positions was to be "by holie

and free election of the Lord's holie people." "Thus hath everie one of the people interest in the election and ordination of their officers."[39]

The pastor is to be chosen by the congregation based on extensive discussion, but not elected by vote. On the one hand, Barrowe condemned democratic election by the membership because in Christ's church "there is no devision in that bodie, neither anything done according to the will of man, but according to the will of God only, all having received of and being guided by one and the same spirit, even as God is one." On the other hand, he insisted "elders are appointed to see the gouernment & order of Christ obserued; not to take yt al into ther hands." In spite of the general apostasy "the companie" still has the "spiritual power of our Lord Jesus Christ . . . to ordain their ministers."[40]

However, once a pastor is chosen, according to John Greenwood (Barrowe's London colleague), the members are bound to "obey him in the Lord" and his duty is to "teach, guide and govern" them. Like Barrowe, Greenwood maintained that "[pastors] are to be chosen & ordeined by all by publike consent and are then diligently & faithfully to execute their office vnto all, not preiudicing the libertie of any."[41] The London group held the ministry in high esteem. They believed that to have a minister is an essential aspect of the apostolic pattern and that without duly-appointed officers sacraments should not be administered. But they did not believe in formal ordination.

As to relations among churches, Barrowe made allowances for general assemblies.[42] Barrowe said that Christ did not give "unto any one church more power or prerogative than unto all other, or set one church above and over another;" however, they should relate to and help one another, especially when it came to appointment of officers.[43]

The London separatists believed Anglican-administered sacraments to be false, but saw no reason for believers' baptism. Greenwood declared, "I am no Anabaptist, I thank God," but like other separatists he declined to have his son baptized in the Church of England.[44] Barrowe distinguished between the external and internal aspects of baptism; it made no difference whether the external baptism was performed in the Church of Rome, since it was incomplete anyway until joined internally to the holiness of a legitimate church. In light of their rejection of Anglican sacraments, there was a tendency among separatists in London not to stress baptism and the Lord's supper.[45]   Indeed, since Barrowe believed the sacraments should be administered only by a pastor, the Barrowists did not administer baptism until Francis Johnson was appointed minister in 1592. In contradistinction from Calvin, the Barrowists maintained that discipline was more important than the sacraments as a mark of the church. For the Barrowists the marks of a true church are discipline, the faith of the members, and a covenant with the Lord.

Vehemently, Barrowe attacked the bishops, blaming them for the unsatisfactory ecclesiastical situation. "We see they bear not Christ's but antichrist's image, mark, life, power."[46] He called Archbishop Whitgift "a monster, a miserable compound . . . neither ecclesiastical, nor civil."[47] As Williams was to do, Barrowe denounced government salaries for the clergy. He disparaged the wealth and social position such support gave them, declaring it contrary to Christ's system of sustenance through free contributions. Government officials found the political overtones of such remarks unacceptable.[48]

Initially Barrowe, like Browne, simultaneously accepted two seemingly irreconcilable notions: an established church and limited magisterial involvement in ministerial affairs. On the one hand, he called upon the queen to suppress any idolatry, including the episcopacy, in order to bring about reform. "Yet now if I be asked who ought to abolish this idolatry, to destroy these synagogues, to dissolve these fraternities, and to depose these antichristian priests: to that I answer, the prince, or state; and that it belongeth not to any private men."[49] No private citizen has the right, he wrote, to "stretch forth their hand by force to the reformation of any public enormities, which are by the magistrate's authority set up."[50] In 1590 Barrowe wrote a detailed guide, entitled The First Part of the Platforme, which explained how Elizabeth should proceed to reform the church, but the tract was rejected by Lord Burghley, and Barrowe was imprisoned.[51] On the other hand, Barrowe's views regarding the role of the magistrate changed prior to his trial; he became convinced that the word of God necessarily limits the queen's ecclesiastical authority. In light of the crown's refusal to heed the demand for reform, he stated withdrawal was the only alternative. "Only the magistrate may" noted Barrowe, "pull down the public monuments of idolatry; yet every private Christian both may, and upon pain of damnation ought to, refrain from public idolatry, or from any thing which is evil in God's eyes."[52] To the extent to which the divine will conflicts with that of the prince, the Lord should be obeyed. True Christians, rather than the sovereign, were to bring about the ideal. In response to the question of whether a secular leader can be excommunicated, Barrowe replied "that the church ought to have iudgmente ready against euery transgression without respect of person, and that the Pastor of the church ought to pronounce it."[53]

At the turn of the century, soon after James I assumed the English throne, separatism crystallized as a notable movement with the conversion of two Anglican ministers to the cause. Disappointed by the new king's response in 1603 to the millenary petition and other puritan demands, John Smyth and John Robinson (c.1575-1625) defected from the established church. A separated conventicle began in 1606 in the village of Scrooby under the leadership of Robinson and Richard Clyfton; the Mayflower Pilgrims who in 1620 established Plymouth, Massachusetts were an offshoot of that congregation.[54] The first English baptists, on the other hand, were members of a group of disserters led by John Smyth--known to posterity as the se-baptist (self-baptist)--originating in the nearby village of Gainsborough.[55]

The first General Baptists were members of Smyth's Gainsborough church. Having emerged from the separatist movement, they afterwards rejected the strict Calvinistic doctrine of election; they believed instead that Christ died for all people, even though many would not be saved. Historically, descendants of the group led by John Smyth are known as General or Armenian Baptists to distinguish them from Particular or Calvinistic Baptists who emerged in the 1630s, and from Continental anabaptists. By rejecting the Reformed doctrine of election and double predestination, the General Baptists put their faith in the general redemption of humanity. They were soteriologically Armenian. The General Baptists' view of the atonement distinguished them from the Particular Baptists who believed in a limited atonement or particular redemption: the doctrine that

Christ died only for the elect--a select number of saints.[56] The baptist movement emerged from within the cradle of separatism. While the baptists were separatists, they were also rebaptizers who considered infant baptism administered by the Church of England inadequate. They believed that there is no scriptural warrant for paedobaptism and that the sacraments should be reserved only for consenting adults. Adult or believers' baptism was not originally part of separatist doctrine.

The origin of the baptist churches both in the old and new worlds is intimately connected with the life and thought of John Smyth. Smyth pioneered a restoration of what many baptists believe to be a New Testament understanding of adult baptism, church polity, and church-state relations, possibly as a result of the influence of the Mennonites with whom he had contact in Holland. In 1608 or 1609 he baptized himself--an act which horrified most of the early separatists as well as Anglicans. Smyth's self-baptism while in Holland marks a turning point in the history of English nonconformity; with it separatism entered a new era by presenting baptism as a voluntary profession of faith. Smyth did not believe that a church is constituted on the basis of a covenant which was the cornerstone of the theology of all early separatists. Rather, he maintained, it was based on believers' baptism. Smyth saw his own and the movement's progression from puritanism to separatism to baptism as a clear act of Divine Providence. Smyth died in Amsterdam in 1612, and his group fragmented, yet many of his beliefs and concerns travelled back to England and on to America during the next three decades. Most subsequent separatists, including Williams after his banishment, followed Smyth's example and rejected paedobaptism.

John Robinson, Francis Johnson, Henry Ainsworth, and Thomas Helwys were contemporaries of Smyth who played major roles in the separatist drama during the early seventeenth century.[57] However, for a variety of reasons, Smyth is a good choice for this book. Even though most Congregational historians have been more interested in Robinson's Pilgrims, Smyth was a bold, interesting, imaginative, and open-minded person who pioneered the transition from separatist to baptist principles. Furthermore, whereas Robinson's theology differs only slightly from that of Henry Barrowe and Robert Browne, Smyth's final doctrinal position marks a fundamental departure from previous dissident thought and seems to have laid the groundwork for the ideological maturation that occurred through Williams and others. In contrast, John Robinson, Francis Johnson, and Henry Ainsworth condemned rebaptism; they thereby lacked that significant experiential-intellectual parallel with Williams's life and precepts. The lives and doctrines of Smyth and Williams were remarkably similar.[58] In Cottons Letter Examined Williams mentions Smyth by name several times.[59]

In 1605 John Smyth organized the Gainsborough community; in 1608 or 1609 be adopted believers' baptism. During that period he wrote three major works: Principles and Inferences Concerning the Visible Church (1606 or 07); Parallels, Censures and Observations (1606 or 07; and The Differences of the Churches of the Seperation (1608).[60] Principles and Inferences focuses on the ecclesiological question of the nature and authority of the true church. An exercise in constructive theology, its tone is non-polemical. Because God alone knows the makeup of the invisible church, the visible or militant church was Smyth's primary concern. It is defined as "two, three, or more Saincts joyned together by covenant with God & themselves, freely to use al the holy things of God, according to the word, for their mutual edification & God's glory." The true church is composed of "saincts," is formed by "a covenant betwixt God and the Saincts," and the "presence of Christ" exists deep within it.[61]

A refutation of Richard Bernard's polemic against separatism entitled The Separatists Schisme, Smyth's Parallels, Censures, and Observations is a defense of the separatist movement. Unlike Principles and Inferences, it is polemical. The false church is depicted as a body which is not in accord with the pattern of the New Testament. The Anglican Church was untrue for several reasons. First, it contained the reprobate. "Wicked men joyned with Godly men in a Church, doe not produce a true Church, but a false Church." To be part of such a mixed body is to be necessarily outside "Christ's Kingdome." Second, "Christ is not their King, seeing he onely ruleth by his own Lawes and Officers, not by Antichristian Lords, and Lawes, such as are their Prelates, and their Officers, Courts, and Canons." Finally, "Christ is not their Prophett to teach them by their false Prophetts the instruments of

Antichrist." For Smyth everything within the Church of England was untrue. Thus, Smyth referred to the Church of England as an ecclesiastical system of "false repentance, false Faith, false Church, false Ministery, false Worship, and false Government." The gathered church receives its authority and autonomy directly from Christ. Further, there is no authority apart from that authorized by the congregation. Any authority that a pastor possesses has been delegated to him by the laity. Parallels, Censures, and Observations clearly indicates that Smyth was a separatist but not yet a baptist, in that he indicated no special interest in the issue of baptism and called the separatist beliefs "the vndoubted truth of God."[62] Moreover, he condemned anabaptism as well as papism:

> Neither can a wicked company be called Holy or Saints truly in respect of the visible signes of Gods favor or presence, For then the Papists, Anabaptists, Familists, Arrians, & other Heretiques should truly be called Saints.[63]

Differences of the Churches of the Separation focuses on use of the scriptures during worship, utilization of prescribed forms of worship, and the authority of church officers. Baptism is not mentioned. Even so, Smyth did argue for spiritual liberty and against prescribed forms of readings, prayer, or worship. "Whither we pray, prophesy, or sing it must be the word of scripture, not out of the book but out of the hart."[64] The Bible used by the pastor should be in the original languages, not a vernacular translation. Smyth decided to sever contact with the Ancient Church until it renounced the "mysterie of iniquitie" in its "worship and offices."[65] Smyth's affirmation in Differences of the Churches is that "wee hould that the worship of the new testament properly so called is spirituall, proceeding originally from the hart: & that reading out of a booke . . . is no part of spiritual worship, but rather the invention of the man of synne."[66] He distinguished between the business or governmental functions of the church and its devotional aspect by referring to the difference between the "kingdom of the saynts" and the "priesthood of the saynts."[67]

In 1608 or 1609 Smyth, having rejected baptism by the Anglican Church, immersed himself and his followers. (In this respect Williams resembled Smyth.) Robinson provides the following account of Smyth's self-baptism: "Mr. Smith, Mr. Helwys, and the rest, having disclaimed their former Church state and ministry came together to erect a new Church by baptism . . . . Mr. Smith baptized first himself, and next Mr. Helwys, and so the rest."[68] This act marks the beginning of the English baptist movement.

Smyth believed that it was inconsistent for separatists who baptized infants to acknowledge only the baptismal practices of the English church while simultaneously condemning every other aspect of that body. Contending that baptism should not be administered to infant children, he criticized Robinsonian separatists for acquiescing to the Anglican baptisms.[69] Smyth's views were a prelude to views espoused later by Williams rejecting not only the English Protestant Church, but all state churches.

A major difference between the baptists and their antipaedobaptist brethren of the separation was that for the former baptism of believers replaced the signed covenant as the sign of membership. Smyth reconstituted his community "on the basis of believers' baptism in the place of a church covenant." For him, a church is constituted on the basis of conversion of truly regenerate adults, not a covenant. Adult baptism is the ultimate profession of repentance and faith, highlighting the distinction from state churches. Consequently many separatists, including Williams, adopted the doctrine of believers' baptism and with it the principle of liberty of conscience.

Three works mark this final baptist stage in Smyth's spiritual development: The Character of the Beast (1609), Propositions and Conclusions Concerning True Christian Religion (1610), and The Last Booke of Iohn Smith, Called the Retraction of His Errours (1612).[70] Asserting that without proper baptism there can be no true church, Smyth contended in The Character of the Beast, as Williams did thirty years later, that acceptance of adult baptism was the logical end result of separatism. Believers' baptism is the foundation of the true apostolic church. The ritual of baptism is the ultimate indication of a free commitment; a church covenant is not sufficient. Smyth contended he had as much right to initiate himself and his followers in accord with New Testament teachings (in order to set up a legitimate church) as the separatists had to break away from the established order in England

and start anew through self-proclaimed covenants. For him infant baptism rather than participating in the worship of a false church was to be rejected as "the character of the beast," i.e., a sin to be renounced before one can be forgiven.[71] Smyth felt the theological movement from puritanism to separatism and then to the baptist movement was predestined by the Lord. "That we should fal from the profession of Puritanisme to Brownisme, & from Brownisme to true Christian baptisme," wrote Smyth, "is not simply evil or reprovable in it self, except it be proved that we have fallen from true religion."[72] Williams afterwards concurred; both he and Smyth went through each of those phases.

Ecclesiologically, Smyth was a congregationalist, yet in this first book after becoming a baptist he attacked the opinions of his separatist friends. Smyth's assault was directed against the inconsistencies of the separatists as well as Anglicans, a factor that did not endear him to his former associates. "Be it knowne . . . to all the Seperation that we account them in respect of their constitution to bee as very an harlot as either her Mother England, or her grandmother Rome is, out of whose loynes she came." Doctrinally and liturgically there were few differences between Smyth and Robinson, but Smyth's baptism was sufficient to differentiate them. Smyth asserted that because the separatists practised the baptism of children they shared "the mark of the beast."

In a debate with Smyth, Richard Clyfton defended baptism of infants. Circumcision, he maintained, was the seal of the Abrahamic covenant for Jews and baptism the mark of the new covenant for Christians. Smyth, on the other hand, distinguished between the covenants between Abraham and the Lord: one with the "carnal seed" sealed by circumcision, the other with the "spiritual seed" consummated by the Holy Spirit. A person "must first beleeve actually then receave the baptisme of water;" he "must bee one that confesseth his Fayth & his sinnes, one that is regenerate & borne againe."[73]

Smyth was convinced that because he lived in an age "when Antichrist hath destroyed the true baptisme. The[n] must we reare it up againe." In The Character of the Beast he justified his unusual personal baptism by declaring that it was essential for the true church to reconstitute "the old Apostolique baptisme which Antichrist had overthrowne."[74] If they have the right to set up true churches, then they are able to establish an authentic form of initiation into the church. He believed in a spiritual, not a literal, baptismal succession. Responding to the accusation that he advocated anabaptism, Smyth wrote that baptism of a child or of any one who has not yet been converted is invalid. Immersion of a voluntary believer is the correct baptismal practice.[75]

Proposition and Conclusions contained the first baptist confession of faith; written in Latin, it consisted of one hundred articles. Articles 12 states: "The Church of Christ is the society of believers who have been baptized after confession of faith and of sins, on which society the power of Christ has been bestowed." Doctrinally its principles are essentially Armenian, not Reformed--the high Calvinist doctrine of double predestination having been rejected in favor of the view that Christ died for everyone. Many are condemned to eternal damnation, but because of their faithlessness, not because God prejudged them or decided by fiat. Everyone has the freedom to choose or reject the Lord.[76] God condemns no one to spiritual death. He called original sin "an idle terme," because it only concerned Adam, not his descendants. For the first time Smyth defended liberty of conscience. The prince should "leaue Christian religion free, to euery mans conscience, and to handle onely ciuil transgressions, injuries and wrongs . . . for Christ only is the King and lawgiver of Church and conscience."[77]

Believers' baptism was an embarrassment to the separatists in that it exposed them to the accusation that they were anabaptists. While his act of self-immersion brought separatism to a new stage, Smyth nonetheless has been remembered as being theologically and emotionally inconsistent. Similar charges of being erratic were lodged in New England against Roger Williams. There are other similarities between Williams and Smyth as well, and the works of Williams parallel Smyth's in a striking manner, as we shall see.

The history of Smyth's life is interesting, but sad. Though charismatic and inspired, he nevertheless seems to have been unstable. In particular, he had difficulty getting along with other separatist leaders and in keeping his followers united. The anarchy predicated by Whitgift as a necessary consequence of sectarianism was manifested clearly in Smyth's group; his congregation experienced considerable strife and ultimately a schism, yet with his self-immersion separatism entered a new stage.

The early separatists, all Englishmen, can only be understood within a Tudor-Stuart context. It would be absurd to contend that the first separatists were apostles of modern democracy as we know it today. They were ardent Calvinists. Any contribution to political democracy was fortuitous. They advocated personal freedom, not universal liberty. In fact, it is ironic that their rigidity helped bring about tolerance, because within their own congregations dissidence was intolerable. Their concern was freedom of worship for themselves, not the rights of others, notwithstanding the tendency of Smyth and the baptists toward individual freedom. Placing the power to discipline in the hands of local congregations and pastors tended, in the short run, to decrease tolerance and increase uniformity insofar as the zeal to ferret out sinners and hypocrites leads to bigotry. Their separation was not intended to bring liberty for all. Tolerance emerged only as an unintended byproduct of efforts to gain freedom for themselves. Still, the nineteenth-century German historian, Ernst Troeltsch, was probably correct to have written that "religious toleration was one logical result of the rise of congregationalism and of the Free Church movement."[78] In the endeavor to find a place where they could worship freely, these ardent Calvinists inadvertently enhanced the liberty of others.

Chapter 4

Endnotes

[1]The traditional interpretation that Browne is the founder of Elizabethan separatism is disputed by B. R. White and Verne Morey. See B. R. White, English Separatist Tradition, 44-45; and Verne D. Morey, "History Corrects Itself: Robert Browne and Congregational Beginnings," Bulletin of the American Congregational Association (January, 1954), V, 9-19.

Only three alternatives seem likely: (a) Browne derived his ideas from the anabaptists, (b) he was influenced either by a proto-separatist group or by the Lollards, or (c) he arrived at the essential principles of separatism through a study of the scriptures and in reaction to the stringent measures of Queen Elizabeth. Though all three alternatives are possible, the latter seems most plausible, and I would contend his contribution to separatism was considerable.

The most famous group holding independent worship services prior to the 1580s was a company of approximately two hundred people who met secretly in London in Plumbers' Hall during the 1560s. Whether they were puritans, separatists, or proto-separatists is debatable.

[2]Browne, Booke Which Sheweth, ed. Peel and Carlson, Writings of Harrison and Browne, 255.

[3]Browne, A Booke Which Sheweth, ed. Peel and Carlson, Writings of Harrison and Browne, 253.

[4]Browne, Booke Which Sheweth, 222-395.

[5]Browne, Trve and Short Declaration, ed. Peel and Carlson, Writings of Harrison and Browne, 420.

[6]Browne, Reformation without Tarying, ed. eel and Carlson, Writings of Harrison and Browne, 166-68.

[7]Ibid., 164 and 168. The prerogative of the magistrate is limited to ruling "the common wealth in all outward iustice."

[8]Ibid., 154-55 and 164. See also 167-68.

[9]Ibid., 158-59.

[10]Browne, Booke which Sheweth, ed. Peel and Carlson, Writings of Harrison and Browne, 281.

[11]Browne, Reformation without Tarying, ed. Peel and Carlson, Writings of Harrison and Browne, 162.

[12]Ibid., 152-53.

[13]Browne, A Briefe Discoverie, ed. Carlson, Writings, 1587-90, III, 546.

[14]Browne, <u>Reformation without Tarying</u>, ed. Peel and Carlson, <u>Writings of Harrison and Browne</u>, 152.

[15]<u>Ibid</u>., 164.

[16]Browne, <u>Booke which Sheweth</u>, ed. Peel and Carlson, <u>Writings of Harrison and Browne</u>, 330.

[17]Frederick Powicke was the first to use the phrase "erastian congregationalist" in <u>Robert Browne</u>, 79. See Browne, <u>Reformation without Tarying</u>, ed. Peel and Carlson, <u>Writings of Harrison and Browne</u>, 167.

[18]Browne, <u>Reformation without Tarying</u>, ed. Peel and Carlson, <u>Writings of Harrison and Browne</u>, 164.

[19]In a 1589 letter to an uncle, Browne declared: "I answere that the Ciuil Magistrate must restraine that licentiousness [of all factions and heresies]." Robert Browne, <u>A "New Years Guift": An Hitherto Lost Treatise by Robert Browne The Father of Congregationalism. In the form of a Letter to his uncle Mr. Flowers</u> (December 31, 1588), ed. Champlin Burrage (London, 1904), 30.

[20]Browne, "Introduction," ed. Peel and Carlson, <u>Writings of Harrison and Browne</u>, 16-17.

[21]Throughout his life, Browne's name remained notorious and was viewed by the enemies of separatism as synonymous with the principles of church organization he first advanced.

[22]Williams, <u>Cottons Letter Examined</u>, ed. Guild, <u>Complete Writings</u>, I, 100.

[23]Barrow, "Barrow's First Examination, November 19, 1587," ed. Leland H. Carlson, <u>The Writings of John Greenwood And Henry Barrow, 1587-1590</u> (London, 1970), III, 96; Barrow, "Barrow's Fourth Examination, March 18, 1588," ed. Carlson, <u>Writings, 1587-90</u>, III, 177 and 188; and Barrow and Greenwood, <u>Writings, 1591-93</u>, VI, 74 and 219.

[24]Williams, <u>Cottons Letter Examined</u>, ed. Guild, <u>Complete Writings</u>, 96-97; Williams, <u>The Bloudy Tenent</u>, ed. Caldwell, <u>Complete Writings</u>, 409; and Williams, <u>Bloody Tenent Yet More Bloody</u>, ed. Caldwell, <u>Complete Writings</u>, 331.

[25]Barrow, <u>A Briefe Discoverie</u>, ed. Carlson, &-<u>Writings, 1587-90</u>, III, 303. This was Barrowe's major work.

[26]<u>Ibid</u>.

[27]<u>Ibid</u>., 347 and 517.

[28]Barrow, "Fourth Examination," ed. Carlson, Writings, 1587-90, III, 188-89.

[29]Greenwood, A Briefe Refutation of Mr. George Giffard ([Dort], 1591), ed. Carlson, Writings of Greenwood and Barrow, VI, 23.

[30]Barrow, "Barrow's Fifth Examination, March 24, 1588," ed. Carlson, Writings, 1587-90, VI, 196.

[31]Ibid.

[32]Barrow, A Brief Summe of the Causes of Our Separation, and of Our Purposes in Practise ([Dort], 1588)," ed. Carlson, Writings, 1587-1590, III, 54, 120, 129, and 179.

[33]Barrowe wrote, "I have already often, and I hope, sufficiently shewed, how corruptly Mr. Calvin thought of the Church, or rather how ignorant he was thereof." Henry Barrow, A Plaine Refutation of Mr. George Giffard's Reprochful Booke, Intituled, A Short Treatise against the Donatists of England ([Dort], 1590), ed. Leland H. Carlson, The Writings of Henry Barrow, 1590-91, V, 163.

[34]Barrow, True Description, ed. Carlson, Writings, 1587-90, III, 214.

[35]Barrow, True Description, ed. Carlson, Writings, 1587-90, III, 214.

[36]Ibid., III, 276.

[37]In 1591, Barrowe wrote that God had called his people "out of the false Church from confusion, and out of the world from dispersion, unto the true Church, unto order." Barrow, A Refutation of Mr. Giffard's Reasons Concerning our Purposes in the Practise of the Truth of the Gospel of Christ ([Dort], 1591), ed. Carlson, Writings, 1590-91, V, 338.

[38]Barrow, Briefe Discoverie, ed. Carlson, Writings, 1587-90, III, 559.

[39]Barrow, True Description, ed. Carlson Writings, 1587-90, III, 216.

[40]Barrow, A Plaine Refutation, ed. Carlson, Writings, 1590-91, V, 146 and 234.

[41]John Greenwood, A Collection of Certaine Sclaunderous Articles Gyven out by the Bisshops ([Dort], 1588), ed. Carlson, Writings of Greenwood, IV, 161.

[42]Williams opposed all synods, including the Westminster Assembly. Cartwright, Browne, and Cotton viewed them as essential.

[43]Barrow, A Plaine Refutation, ed. Carlson, Writings, 1590-91, V, 147.

[44]Greenwood, "Greenwood's Examination, March 24, 1588," ed. Carlson, Writings of Greenwood, IV, 26.

[45]Greenwood, An Answere to George Gifford's Pretended Defence of Read Praiers and Devised Litourgies ([Dort], 1590), ed. Carlson, Writings of Greenwood, IV, 77.

[46]Barrow, A Plaine Refutation, ed. Carlson, Writings, 1590-91, V, 258-59. See also pages 265-66.

[47]Barrow, "Barrow's Fourth Examination," ed. Carlson, Writings, 1587-90, III, 188.

[48]Barrowe refused to worship at the official parish church, to pay tithes, to swear any oath, to obey the laws requiring eating fish during Lent, and to recognize the legitimacy of the Church of England.

[49]Barrow, Briefe Discoverie, ed. Carlson, Writings, 1587-90, III, 629.

[50] Barrow, The First Part of the Platforme, Penned by that worthy servant of Jesus Christ, and Blessed witnes of his most Holy Ordinances, to the Losse of Life: Mr. Henry Barrowe ([Dort], 1590), ed. Carlson, Writings, 1587-90, III, 229.

[51]Ibid., III, 239.

[52]Barrow, A Briefe Discoverie, ed. Carlson, Writings, 1587-90, III, 481.

[53]Barrow, A Plaine Refutation, ed. Carlson, Writings, 1587-90, V, 40 and 158.

[54]In Yet More Bloody, Williams refers to a letter from Robinson to the colony in Plymouth, Massachusetth. Williams, Bloody Tenent Yet More Bloody, ed. Caldwell, Complete Writings, IV, 316-17. Robinson is also mentioned to Williams, Cottons Letter Answered, ed. Guild, Complete Writings, I, 102.

[55]Smyth is cited in Williams, Cottons Letter Examined, ed. Guild, Complete Writings, I, 57-59 and 343.

[56]Arminianism, named after Jacob Arminius (1560-1609), represents a significant response to the rigid predestinarianism of high Calvinism. It is the belief that God loves all people and that Christ died for all, though not everyone will be saved. The Calvinistic belief that most people are predestined to damnation was rejected by Arminius in favor of the view that Christ died for all humanity though only the faithful gain from the Lord's sacrifice.
    The implication of such a view is that man has the power to do something to ensure his own salvation. Salvation depends on man's response as well as on God's grace. Although God has a foreknowledge of the way in

which men will respond to grace, He does not determine precisely how they will react, thus grace may be lost.

[57]Johnson and Ainsworth were followers of Barrowe who became leaders of the exiled Barrowist church in Amsterdam. Williams mentions Ainsworth in Cottons Letter Examined and praises his book, Annotations of the Five Books of Moses, in Bloudy Tenent. Williams, Cottons Letter Examined, ed. Guild, Complete Writings, I, 98; and Williams, Bloudy Tenent, ed. Caldwell, Complete Writings, III, 308.
Helwys was one of Smyth's closest followers, but when Smyth sought to join the Waterland Mennonite Church, Helwys and a few others in Smyth's congregation broke relations with Smyth and returned to London to found the first baptist church on English soil.

[58]As William Warren Sweet indicated in Religion in Colonial America, "Roger Williams was the John Smith of America and like the father of the English Baptists passed through several states of religious change." William Warren Sweet, Religion in Colonial America (New York, 1942), 122.

[59]Williams, Cottons Letter Examined, ed. Guild, Complete Writings, I, 57-59 and 343.

[60]John Smyth, Principles and *Inferences* Concerning the Visible Church, ed. Whitley, Works of John Smyth, I, 249-68; John Smyth, Parallels, Censures and Observations, ed. Whitley, Works of John Smyth; II, 327-562; and John Smyth, Differences of the Churches of the Seperation, ed. Whitley, Works of John Smyth, I, 269-320.

[61]Smyth, Principles and Inferences, ed. Whitley, Works of John Smith, I, 252.

[62]Smyth, Parallels, Censures, ed. Whitley, Works of John Smyth, II, 354, 357, 468, 468, 515-16, 135, and 35.

[63]Ibid., 343.

[64]Smyth, Differences of the Churches, ed. Whitley, Works of John Smyth, I, 303.

[65]Ibid., i.

[66]Smyth, Differences of the Churches, ed. Whitley, Works of John Smyth, I, v.

[67]Ibid., 125.

[68]Robinson, Of Religious Communion, ed. Ashton, Works, III, 48. Cf. Smyth, The Character of the Beast (Amsterdam, 1609), ed. Whitley, Works of John Smyth, II, 660.

[69]For Smyth it was illogical to retain as the basis for church membership a sacrament derived from a false church and to reject all aspects of Anglicanism except its method of baptism.

[70]John Smyth, The Character of the Beast (1609), ed. Whitley, Works of John Smyth, II, 563-680; Smyth, Propositions and Conclusions Concerning True Christian Religion Conteyning a Confession of Faith of Certaine English People, Living at Amsterdam (Amsterdam, 1610), ed. Whitley, Works of John Smyth, II, 733-50; and John Smyth, The Last Booke of John Smith, Called the Retraction of His Errours, and the Confirmation of the Truth (Amsterdam 1612), ed. Whitley, Works of John Smyth, II, 751-760. By the word "character" Smyth means mark.

[71]Smyth, Character of the Beast, ed. Whitley, Works of John Smyth, II, 593.

[72]Ibid.

[73]Smyth, Character of the Beast, ed. Whitley, Works of John Smyth, II, 579, 582, and 611-12.

[74]Ibid., II, 657 and 659.

[75]Ibid., 655.

[76]Smyth, Propositions and Conclusions, ed. Whitley, Works of John Smyth, II, 734-37.

[77]Ibid., 734-37, 748, and 757.

[78]Ernst Troeltsch, The Social Teaching of the Christian Churches (New York, 1960; German edition, 1911), II, 671.

CHAPTER V
SEPARATIST CONTEMPORARIES

To understand Williams's views within the context of history, it is necessary to discuss contemporary separatist and baptist thought in England and America during the Cromwellian decades.[1] The revolutionary age is important for a variety of reasons: Williams returned to talk with some old friends across the sea during that time, Williams was intricately involved in the drama which unfolded in the motherland, and widespread pleas for toleration (of sectarians at the very least, but even of Quakers, Catholics, Jews, and Turks) were heard for the first time with the summoning of the puritan-controlled Long Parliament in 1640. Prior to the 1640s, separatists and baptists were an oppressed minority operating underground within the society. The eruption of hostilities ended that state of repression and produced for them a newfound freedom. The Civil War allowed them the opportunity to merge from the underground and to proclaim their views openly.

Several of Williams's separatist contemporaries will be mentioned in this chapter.[2] The most significant separatist with whom Williams came into contact during his trips to England was John Canne, Ainsworth's successor as minister of the Ancient Church in Amsterdam. The career of Canne is indicative of the history of seventeenth-century separatism; he was successively a puritan, a separatist, possibly a baptist, and during the 1650s a Fifth Monarchist. During the 1620s Canne was pastor of a separatist congregation in ante-bellum London which had been founded in 1621 by John Hubbard.[3] From 1630 (or '31) until 1647 (or '48) Canne was exiled in Holland where he led the remnants of Ainsworth's Ancient Church and operated a printshop that published dissident works. In a work written in 1656 he described that period as "seventeen years' banishment" for him.[4] In Early English Dissenters Champlin Burrage wrote that after "Ainsworth died in 1622 . . . There was no pastor or teacher in the congregation [in Amsterdam] until after the arrival of John Canne about 1630.[5] In 1632, one year after Williams arrived in Boston, Canne published his first work, The Way to Peace: or, Good Counsel for it. Regarding Canne's attempt to heal the wounds of the past, Burrage has observed that "the mere title [of Canne's book] perhaps gives us the most suggestive and important point of all, namely, that Canne may temporarily have succeeded in healing the long standing breach between [Jean] de l'Ecluse and [Sabine] Staresmore," two members of the Ancient Church.[6] Historian John Wilson declared that "Canne was able temporarily to reunite the Ainsworth old church, but that the reconciliation was not permanent."[7] In Amsterdam Canne's press published many nonconformist tracts, and he is best known for his annotated Bible. In the late 1640s he returned to warn-torn England.

Abruptly, Canne became a leading spokesman for the separatist cause when, in 1634, he published his most influential work, A Necessitie of Separation from the Church of England, proved by the Nonconformists Principles. In A Necessitie of Separation, Canne sought to demonstrate the connection between separatism and puritanism, insisting that the principles of nonconformity necessarily lead to a policy of separation. He declared that the non-separating congregationalists held the same views as the separatists, but failed to adhere to their convictions and follow their ideas to their logical conclusion.[8] Having read A Necessitie of Separation, in 1644 Williams wrote in Cottons Letter Examined:

> I believe that there hardly hath ever been a conscientious Separatist who was not first a puritan; for (as Mr. Canne hath unanswerably proved) the grounds and principles of the puritans against bishops and ceremonies . . . must necessarily, if truly followed, lead on to and enforce a separation from such ways, worships, and worshippers.[9]

In 1639 Canne wrote A Stay against Straying in which he argued--contrary to Robinson, yet in agreement with Williams--that true believers should not listen to Anglican preachers.[10] Canne contended that various saints were at that time receiving revelations from God that explained the meaning of biblical prophecies. In point of fact, fourteen years later he announced he was such a prophet who was called to act for the "fulfilling of the will and commandement of God."[11] Furthermore, he maintained that true spirituality included outward actions as well as inner piety and necessitated reformation of patterns of worship in addition to personal piety. In 1642 Necessitie of Separation and A Stay Against Straying were both attacked by the puritan divine John Ball who called Canne "the leader of the English Brownists in Amsterdam."[12]

Canne's view on church-state relations was that the elect should render to Caesar that which is political, that civil authorities should not interfere in ecclesiastical concerns, and that the authorities have no right to coerce anyone to attend a particular church. At the same time he still believed that the state has the right to support a true church. That is to say, like Cartwright, Browne, and Cotton before him, Canne had not abandoned the Old Testament model and thus contrary to Williams did not advocate separation of church and state.

Some historians have sought to prove that from 1640 until 1647 Canne was a baptist, claiming that in 1640 he preached to a congregation of baptists in Broadmead. In E. B. Underhill's Records of a Church of Christ meeting in Broadmead, Bristol, 1640-1687 Canne is called a "baptized man."[13] W. K. Jordan observed in Development of Religious Toleration in England that "Canne was of a mercurial temperament and had soon embraced Baptist doctrines with a large group in the congregation . . . . and set up a new congregation with Baptist leanings, and the Elder de l'Ecluse was chosen pastor of the parent church." Jordan regards him "as a congregationalist before 1640, and a Baptist thereafter."[14] However, Burrage has shown that Canne was neither a baptist nor an anabaptist. The documentation for Burrage's conclusion is in an article entitled, "Was John Canne A Baptist?" Challenging Underhill's sources as unhistorical, Burrage says that Canne never visited Bristol before 1648, that he never was a baptist, and that he was a millenarian (a proto-Fifth Monarchist) instead during the 1640s.[15] Wilson agrees with Burrage's assessment, contending that "John Canne begins to come into focus as a credible figure who moved directly from Separatism into

Millenarian agitation without passing through a Baptist phase."[16] Wilson believes that Canne's apocalyptic interpretation of scripture is the key to understanding his career.

During the 1650s Canne became in England a leading figure in the movement for erection of the chiliastic Fifth Monarchy. The Fifth Monarchists were millenarians who during the interregnum anticipated and attempted to bring about the long awaited thousand-year reign of the saints. They believed that the Fourth Monarchy was coming to an end to be replaced with rule by God's elect. Their views were the antithesis of those that Williams espoused in the 1650s; they were unwilling to await the advent of the millennium quietly, rather they sought its arrival actively. Hence, the Fifth Monarchists endeavored to impose their views on the entire nation (and thus discipline the ungodly) by gaining control over the government and using the power of the state for religious purposes. In 1653 Canne served as chaplain to Colonel Robert Overton, the governor of Hull, Later he became involved in a controversy in that city with John Shaw, a Presbyterian minister, and in 1656 the municipal authorities barred Canne from holding worship services and ordered him to leave town, apparently because of his Danielic Monarchist views.[17] Fifth Monarchy men argued for a rule of the elect, rather than for religious liberty. They believed that they could help usher in the reign of Christ through political action. The extent to which they advocated violent overthrow of the government differed from person to person. Whereas Williams advocated purely spiritual solutions, they did not. For instance, a group of Monarchists declared in a manifesto written in 1649 that they anticipated that Christ would establish a kingdom that was "external and visible."[18]

In 1644 Canne's ideas about separatism were generally in accord with those of Williams, but that was no longer true twelve years later because Canne had become an avid Fifth Monarchist. Though Canne still considered himself a separatist, by 1656 he was a leading figure in the movement to establish a disciplined godly commonwealth ruled by the saints.[19] In 1657 he penned The Time of the End which included prefaces written by two other preachers associated with the Fifth Monarchy, John Rogers and Christopher Feake. In that pamphlet Canne interpreted various apocalyptic passages of scripture, including Daniel's vision of the last days (Daniel 10-12). Canne declared that the millennium was near, that son the saints would attack Babylon, and that the "Beast" was "a State or Government set up by a few apostates"--possibly a veiled reference to the Cromwellian Protectorate. While preaching in April 1658 at a meetinghouse on Swan Alley in London, Canne and seven members of the congregation were arrested, thrown into prison, but he was later acquitted by the courts. In 1658 he and several other Fifth Monarchists wrote A Narrative of their sufferings.[20] With the recall of the Rump Parliament in 1659, Canne served as the regime's official newswriter from May to August, editing two government newspapers until the collapse of the Commonwealth. Because the administration of Charles II proved less tolerant of Fifth Monarchy views, in 1660 Canne fled again to Amsterdam. In 1662 he published an annotated Bible.

In order to understand Canne and separatism in general, another group--the Levellers--needs briefly to be mentioned. The Levellers were a group of "populists" who functioned somewhat like a political party fighting for political democracy. D. B. Robertson has characterized the Levellers as "the radical political party in the New Model Army in and around London during the period between 1647 and 1649."[21] Michael Watts has written that some of the Leveller leaders and many of their followers were religiously separatists, observing that two of the three principal Leveller pamphleteers, John Lilburne and Richard Overton, were for extended periods of time members of separated churches, and the third, William Walwyn, advocated toleration for the separatists.

John Lilburne (1615-1675) was the most significant leader in this famous "people's party."[22] Originally a clothier's apprentice, during the war Lilburne rose to the position of lieutenant-colonel in the Parliamentary army, but in 1645 he had a falling out with the House of Commons under whose service he had been fighting and was imprisoned. For many years he was imprisoned and twice he was tried for treason, but acquitted. After his release from prison in 1640 he joined th separatist church of Edmund Rosier.[23] In 1655, after being imprisoned again. Lilburne became a Quaker, renouncing use of all weapons except the sword of the Spirit. He described his conversion in a 1656 tract entitled The Resurrection of John Lilburne, now a prisoner in Dover Castle.24

A vehement anti-cleric, Lilburne believed in dissociation with the Church of England, but not in Williams's doctrines of religious liberty and separation of church and state. Nor did Lilburne believe in religious toleration. He alleged that the Anglican Church was false, an outgrowth of Romanism, and a creature of Antichrist. He said the saints must completely separate from the national church and worship in autonomous groups in accord with individual conscience. As did Williams, Lilburne said that the saints should not listen to the sermons of the false Anglican preachers. He was convinced that the bishops were on the side of Antichrist and that there was an elect group inside the established church, which included himself, willing to fight on behalf of Christ. Lilburne agreed with separatist policies regarding church membership and use of a covenant, indeed with the separatist doctrine of the church in general. In A Copie of a Letter . . . to Mr. William Prinne, Esq. Lilburne attacked non-separating Independency.25

Eventually, the Leveller-sectarian alliance disintegrated on account of Leveller rebellions within the New Model Army and for other reasons. After the Levellers mutinied in several regiments of the New Model Army, Cromwell turned against them, squelching their revolt with a surprise attack at Burford in 1649. Parliament had declared such revolts within the army to be treason. During this time the antagonism between Lilburne and Cromwell grew. In 1649 the Council of State tried Lilburne for high treason, but he was acquitted.

According to one historian, in Lilburne's eyes "the sectarian coup de grace was administered by his old publisher and patriarch of the Separatist cause, John Canne, lately returned from Amsterdam and now in government employ."26 In The Golden Rule Canne defended the right of Parliament to punish Charles I for treason in 1649. Although Canne had published several separatist works while in Amsterdam, during the civil war he was employed by Parliament. For instance, he penned three tracts justifying the policy of the Commonwealth against the presbyterians, the Irish, the Scots, and Levellers, all of which were published by the government. Canne was probably one of the authors of The Discoverer, a tract attacking the "destructive design" of the Levellers, but not criticizing gathered churches and their right to choose their own ministers.[27] Lilburne believed it was written principally by Canne; a seventeenth century book seller, George Thomason, concurred that it was Canne's handiwork.[28] After the incident at Burford, Lilburne called Canne "that apostate, John Canne" and his congregations "the pretended churches of God, either Independent or Anabaptist." Canne had broken with the Levellers after Burford--even though Canne's press in Amsterdam apparently had printed some of Lilburne's prison writings during the early 1640s.[29]

While in England, Williams was in contact also with non-sectarians. In addition to baptists, Fifth Monarchy men, and various separatists, Williams interacted with Presbyterians, Independents, and the over-all leadership of the Parliamentary cause. Even the Presbyterian scholar Robert Baillie (1599-1662) called Williams "my good acquaintance," even though he was appalled by many of the views of the author of The Bloody Tenent.[30] The non-separating puritans consisted of both Presbyterians and Independents. The sectarians included separatists, baptists, seekers, Quakers, Levellers, Diggers, Ranters, and Fifth Monarchists. The latter four groups sought political solutions, many of them having earlier seceded from separatist, baptist, or even non-separating independent churches. W. Clark Gilpin claims that many of them may have been "offshoots of the church gathered by Henry Jacob in 1616."[31]

Another influential contemporary of Williams was Dr. John Clarke, the Particular Baptist leader who was a founder of Portsmouth, Rhode Island. Born in Suffolk, England, Clarke was educated as a physician, but is best known as a preacher and linguist. In November 1637 Clarke arrived in Boston from England, but soon became disillusioned with the leadership. The antinomian controversy had just concluded in Boston, and he decided to leave the Bay colony the next spring with the expelled Anne Hutchinson and her followers. In search of religious freedom, the antinomian exiles, including the Calvinistic Clarke, first went to New Hampshire, but because the climate was severe they turned southward toward Providence, the home of Roger Williams.[32] Williams, who had arrived two years earlier, helped them to buy land from the Narragansett Indians on the island of Aquidneck (subsequently renamed Rhode Island). In 1638 the town of Portsmouth was established, and one year later Newport. Prior to leaving Boston, on 7 March 1638, Clarke and eighteen other members of the Hutchinson group had signed a document known today as the Portsmouth Compact which pledged "in the presence of Jehovah, to incorporate ourselves into a body politic, and as he shall help us, will submit our persons, lives and estates, unto our Lord Jesus Christ . . . and to all those most perfect and absolute laws of his."[33] They contended that they had divine sanction for their plan for "a democracy, or popular government." The Portsmouth Compact views each citizen as self-governing. Its stress on Christ alone as Lord seems to imply that within the community no human is acknowledged as superior to any other. The state is perceived in that historic covenant as the instrument through which self-government is achieved and religious and civil liberty maintained. The settlers incorporated themselves "into a Bodie Politick" in order to assure self-rule. The compact guarded liberty of conscience, saying no one was "to be accounted a delinquent for doctrine." The magistrate was to punish only "breaches of the law of God that tend to civil disturbance," even though he is the means by which the state enforces the law and protects society.[34]

Whether Clarke, like Williams, was a separatist before arriving in New England is contestable. Some historians have contended he was. For example, Albert H. Newman has written that he "left England as a persecuted separatist;" The Dictionary of Religious Biography says that he "formed Separatist convictions in England;" and three noted church historians have observed that prior to arriving in Boston Clark "had already reached a separatist position."[35] William McLoughlin contends that "the church he [Clarke] led in Portsmouth (and after 1639 in Newport) probably was a Separatist Congregational church until 1644."[35]

In the 1640s the predestinarian Clarke became a baptist, or more correctly an antipaedobaptist. Condemning baptism of infants, Clarke insisted on believers' baptism. Newman has written that Clarke was a Particular Baptist "certainly by 1644, when Mark Lukar, an antipaedobaptist, became associated with him in a church at Newport."[37] Whether he was among those in Rhode Island described by Winthrop as "turned professed anabaptists" in 1641 is uncertain.[38] While living in the Netherlands in the early 1630s, he may have been influenced by the Mennonites. Regardless, by 1644 Clarke's church in Newport became baptist, approximately five years after Williams organized a baptist congregation in Providence in 1639. He served as minister of that congregation--the First Baptist Church of Newport--until his death more than thirty years later. McLoughlin has said that "it may be that the immigration of some Baptists from London, like Henry Lukar, influenced Clark's decision to found a Baptist church but there is no record of this."[39] In 1656 the Second Church of Newport was formed by a splinter group which advocated the laying on of hands.

In 1652 Clarke sailed with Williams to England to obtain a new charter for the colony of Rhode Island which would assure religious freedom as well as confirm the land grant. After nearly twelve years Clarke obtained it form King Charles II; the following year, 1664, he returned to Rhode Island. The charter guaranteed religious liberty to the residents of the colony, and as long as they did not disturb the civil peace, the document specified that they would be free to practice their faith as they pleased: "No person within the said colony, at any time hereafter, shall be anywise molested, punished, disquieted, or called in question, for any differences of opinion on matters of religion."[40]

A year before the Clarke-Williams trip to England, William Witter (1584-1659) asked Clarke's Newport Church to send representatives to his home in Lynn, Massachusetts to baptize some of his neighbors. In response to the call, Clarke and two other baptists, Obadiah Holmes and John Crandall, travelled from Rhode Island to Massachusetts to save some souls. However, while conducting an unauthorized worship service on 20 July 1651, at Witter's home, the three itinerant preachers were arrested by the local constable. Clarke and his two associates were forced to attend the worship services of the Congregational church in Lynn, but when they refused to remove their hats and spoke out against infant baptism during the service they were taken to Boston where they were summarily tried and convicted by Governor John Endecott and the General Court of Massachusetts of the following offenses: preaching without licenses; denying the lawfulness of infant baptism; re-baptizing people; attacking the official form of church polity; administering communion to persons not entitled to it; disturbing the congregation during worship and leaving their hats on in church. For these crimes, all three were briefly imprisoned and fined, and Holmes was shipped.[41] In August 1651 Williams wrote a letter to Endecott condemning the way in which Massachusetts's authorities handled the incident.[42] The next year Clarke described the Witter incident in a treatise published in London entitled Ill Newes from New-England: or a Narative of New-Englands Persecution. In that noteworthy little book, Clarke presented his "testimony" of the "tragicall story" of how he and his friends were mistreated by the authorities in Massachusetts in July of 1651. Clarke described the system in Massachusetts as "false," "evil," and "that which in scripture language is called Babel . . . yea, Antichristian."[43] Quoting the book of Psalms, he asserted that all those who recognize the truth of believers' baptism should "come out from among them (Oh, my people) and be ye separate from them."[44]

Ill Newes from New-England is concerned with the same issues that Williams addressed. It sought, unsuccessfully, to convince Parliament to compel Massachusetts to abide by a policy of religious liberty, and was one of New England's earliest and most important defenses of the right to live in accord with one's conscience. Though overshadowed by his more famous colleague from Rhode Island, Clarke deserves credit for his advocacy of religious liberty as early as the 1650s. Clarke, like Williams, condemned conversion of the Jews by force.[45]

Clarke's words are neither as profound, extensive, nor lucid as those of williams, yet he furthered the cause of liberty. Clarke believed that governments should tolerate religious diversity. Only because he was convinced that the baptist position was the true one, however, did Clarke accentuate the need for freedom for all. Clarke deduced that in any open inquiry believers' baptism would prove to be the true Christian faith. In 1651 Clarke said to the magistrates in Massachusetts that "I desire liberty by the word of God to oppose the faith and order which you profess, thereby to try whether I may be an instrument in the hand of God to remove you from the same."[46]

At the conclusion of Ill Newes from New-England, Clarke presented theological reasons for religious liberty, declaring that "no servant of Christ

Jesus hath any liberty, much less authority, from his Lord to smite his Fellow-servants" and that "this outward forcing of men in matters of conscience towards God to believe as others believe . . . cannot stand with the Peace, Liberty, Prosperity, and safety of a Place, Commonwealth, or nation."[47] For Clarke, no servant of Christ "can have either liberty or authority from him [the Lord] thus to force another mans conscience." For in Ill Newes he said "by outward force to seek to constrain, or restrain an others conscience in the worship of God, & c. doth presuppose one man to have dominion over another mans conscience." "The great work of ordering the understanding and conscience is reserved in His [the Lord's] own hand, and in the hand of the Spirit."[48]

Clarke tried to convince Parliament to allow the tares to grow up with the wheat prior to the "harvest" of the Last Days "lest while ye gather up the tares, ye root up also the wheat with them," as Christ commanded. For him, the tares are "the children of the wicked one" who "afterwards [are] discovered to be Hereticks, Schismaticks, Apostats, Demas, and such false teachers as Peter speacks of, 2 Pet. 2.12."[49]

Ill Newes from New-England provides insight into Clarke's overall doctrinal position, especially his stress on believers' baptism. Theologically Clarke was a Calvinist. He accepted the limited atonement doctrine of the Particular Baptists rather than the Armeninian views of the General Baptists. Clarke advocated adult baptism by immersion and admission of only true believers to worship services, maintaining that the leaders in Massachusetts have no "precept from Christ" either to justify paedobaptism or the use of "the civil sword to correct errour, heresies, and all false worships." "Every creature to whom the Gospel was to be preached," declared Clarke in support of his position, "was by the preaching thereof to be made a disciple before he was to be baptized."[50]

Three other contemporary figures are worthy of note: Sir Henry Vane (1613-1662) who was a close friend of Williams, John Saltmarsh (d. 1647) who was a chaplain in the New Model Army, and John Jackson who probably was a leader of the mystical group known as the seekers. All three were spiritualists.

The most radical sectarians, including Williams, attacked the Westminster Assembly which met in 1643 and the Solemn League and Covenant with the Scottish nation adopted by Parliament in September of that year. Henry Vane the younger, a statesman and diplomat, was one of the three commissioners who negotiated that treaty with Scotland. At that time Vane was serving as an assistant to Parliamentary leader, John Pym (1584-1643). Williams entered full force into the controversy in 1644 with publication of Queries of Highest Consideration.

In 1636, at the age of twenty-three, Sir Henry Vane was made governor of Massachusetts Bay, only a few months after arriving in the colony. In 1637 he lost to John Winthrop in the magisterial election, after having been involved in the antinomian controversy precipitated by Anne Hutchinson and John Wheelwright. Even though his father had been Secretary of State under Charles I, during the 1640s and '50s the younger Vane was an influential leader of the Parliamentary sectarians and friend of Williams. In 1643 as Parliament's ambassador to Scotland, he and two others negotiated the Solemn League and Covenant. That same year he helped Williams obtain a charter for the Providence Plantations. Initially Vane was an associate of Oliver Cromwell, but in 1653 he was expelled from the Rump Parliament for having upset the Lord Protector. After Cromwell's death, however, in 1659 Sir Henry returned as a member of the House of Commons. He was then made a member of the Council of State and of the Committee of Public Safety which reviewed the cases of "persons who continue committed for conscience-sake."[51] But Vane was later imprisoned, having opposed the leadership of Cromwell's son, Richard, and having generated hostility in Parliament because of his friendship with and support for the Fifth Monarchists. When the Stuart monarchy was restored in 1660, he was imprisoned again and two years later beheaded, despite the fact that he had opposed the execution of Charles I.

Vane's religious attitudes are more difficult to determine. His faith was highly mystical, even though his stress on religious toleration is clear. Nowhere in his writings does Vane clearly support all the doctrines of the Fifth Monarchists, although in 1655 in one tract he demonstrated considerable sympathy with many of their ideas and predicted the imminent coming of a Christian theocracy on earth.[52] P. G. Rogers declared in The Fifth Monarchy Men that Vane "was undoubtedly a millenarian like Goffe, and was moreover, on close and friendly terms with persons like John Rogers who were leading exponents of the Fifth Monarchy faith."[53] In 1656 Sir Henry wrote A Healing Question propounded and Resolved, which sought to provide a basis for an alliance between the Fifth Monarchy men and Commonwealth men. He proposed "all honest men within the three nations" who believed in "the good old cause" be united through an elected assembly. Reconciliation never occurred, in part because Vane advocated doctrines which were unacceptable to the Fifth Monarchists. For example, he included the belief that "fundamentals" (i.e., a written constitution) should be adopted to restrain rulers. A few months after publication A Healing Question Propounded and Resolved was declared seditious by the Protectorate, and Vane was imprisoned.[54] While in prison, he became friends with a major leader among the Fifth Monarchists, John Rogers. Vane highlighted the indwelling of the Holy Spirit within each believer in the last days, indicating his antinomian tendencies. Believing that the visible church had been destroyed in the fourth century by the apostasy of the papacy, Vane contended that it would be replaced by a spiritual, not an earthly, ministry. Unlike Williams, however, his vision of the millennium was of a "dispensation in Spirit."[55] As this suggests, doctrinally Vane's spiritualistic ideas were similar to those of the Quakers. For that reason, Vane was more sympathetic toward their beliefs than Williams who vehemently opposed the Friends theologically, even though he supported their civil rights.

John Saltmarsh was a Cambridge-educated clergyman who, in the early 1640s, was made pastor of a rectory in Kent by Parliament. During the period between 1645 and 1647 he wrote twelve works. In 1646 Saltmarsh became a chaplain in a New Model Army under the command of Sir Thomas Fairfax. In 1647 he pleaded with Cromwell on behalf of a group of Levellers imprisoned for mutiny. Saltmarsh, like Vane, was a mystic or spiritualist. William Haller has observed, "There could be no mistaking the antecedents of Saltmarsh's ideas. They were in line with the Theologia Germanica and the sixteenth-century Continental mystics."[56]

In Holy Discoveries and Flames, written in 1640, Saltmarsh described his conversion to puritanism, declared that universal love should be the basis for the brotherhood of man, and warned against the consequences of war. In 1646 in Gangraena the Presbyterian divine Thomas Edwards attacked Saltmarsh. Saltmarsh replied a few months later in Groanes for Liberty and one year later in Reasons for Unitie, Peace, and Love. Saltmarsh sought to achieve "unity of believers" of all kinds, advocating tolerance for the English sectarians-- separatists, baptists and seekers but not for others. He also argued for a lay ministry.[57]

Unlike Williams who was still searching, Saltmarsh claimed that he had discovered the original apostolic pattern of worship and organization, contending that it was purely spiritual. Saltmarsh maintained that a spiritual kingdom would be established within the hearts of the elect at the time of the millennium due to the advent of the Holy Spirit. He rejected any separatist search for the New Testament polity, maintaining that the ideal pattern of church government had been destroyed forever.[58] Saltmarsh rejected the contention of Williams that a true church would exist only after the apostolic ministry is restored. Rather he was convinced restoration would occur with Christ's return in spirit to "the Saints or all true Christians."[59] His opponents, probably correctly, accused him of antinomianism, due to his stress on grace and refusal to obey external laws. Edwards complained that Saltmarsh believed in "free grace" and that men should be judged "according to their heart."[60] Indeed, Saltmarsh was convinced that the reign of God would eventually be realized.

The seekers concluded, according to one scholar, "that the powers and authority granted to the apostles in the New Testament had been so corrupted and destroyed by the Church of Rome that no true church could be constituted until God had raised up a new race of apostles."[61] Convinced that no existing church was truly Christian, the seekers awaited the establishment of the original, apostolic pattern that would accompany the advent of the millennium. Meanwhile, they worshipped Christ in an inward manner. Antinomian ideas were common among seekers. William Braithwaite contends that by the middle of the seventeenth century, seekerism became an aspect of Quakerism, a theological move anathema to

Williams. Watts has said that many seekers as well as baptists and Ranters become Quakers.[62]

Recently, J. F. McGregor has questioned the existence of the seekers as a distinct, organized sect. McGregor's contention is that "there is little objective evidence that either Seekers or Ranters formed coherent movements or that they existed in any considerable numbers . . . they are largely artificial products of the Puritan heresiographers' methodology."[63] Yet, although evidence regarding the seekers is not extensive, several primary sources, including those noted above, mention them by name. Even McGregor acknowledges that there is a "little evidence." For example, Saltmarsh observed that "by 1646 the seekers were a sect fourth in importance only to the Presbyterians, Independents, and Baptists."[64] In 1646 Edwards bemoaned the rapid growth of the seekers. "Very many of the Anabaptists are now turned seekers'," agreed fellow presbyterian Robert Baillie. "including Lawrence Clarkson and Roger Williams."[65] For McGregor, the seekers "are largely artificial products of the Puritan heresiographers' methodology," yet in the same article McGregor contradicts his denial of "the alleged Seekers" by discussing in detail their religious views based on the writings of such seventeenth century contemporaries as John Saltmarsh, Richard Baxter, Thomas Edwards, Laurence Clarkson, William Walwyn, and William Erbery.

Whether John Jackson was a leader of the seekers is uncertain.[66] Nevertheless, prior to Williams's second visit to England, in 1651 Jackson wrote in A Sober Word to a Serious People that he could not see "sufficient ground" for the practices of "the present churches," For Jackson, unless the ministry is truly apostolic it is "giftless." He opposed forming churches on the basis of covenants. Jackson said that such gathered churches were "without precedent from the Word of God." The "work of the ministry," he contended, must be "again restored until its pristine and primitive constitution" in order to accomplish "the end for which Christ ascended."[67]

Chapter 5

Endnotes

[1]In England during the civil war the various religious leaders and groups aligned themselves with either one side or the other. Though differing in objectives and policies, initially most baptists and separatists as well as Presbyterians and Independents supported Parliament's rebellion against Charles I.

[2]Cromwell and Milton will not be discussed, since they were not separatists.

[3]John Wilson and W. E. Axon have said that Canne probably died in Amsterdam in 1667. John F. Wilson, "Another Look at John Canne," Church History, XXXIII (1964), 34-37; and W. E. Axon, "John Canne," ed. Leslie Stephen and Sidney Lee, The Dictionary of National Biography (Oxford, 1917), III, 863.

[4]John Canne, Truth with Time: or, Certain Reasons proving that none of the seven last plagues, or vials, are yet poured out (London, 1656), as cited in Axon, 864. See also John Canne, A Necessitie of Separation from the Church of England, proved by the Nonconformists Principles (Amsterdam, 1634), ed. Charles Stovel (London, 1849), v.

[5]Champlin Burrage, The Early English Dissenters in the Light of Recent Research (1550-1641), I, 172-73. See also Alice C. Carter, The English Reformed Church in Amsterdam (Amsterdam, 1964), 15-20.

[6]Burrage, Early English Dissenters, 178. See also John Canne, The Way to Peace: or, Good Counsel for it . . . at the reconciliation of certain brethren between whom there had been former differences (London, 1632); Benjamin Hanbury, Historical Memorials, I, 516; and John Paget, A Defence of Chvrch-Government, which was published posthumously, Paget wrote, "Mr. Canne . . . [was] rashly elected a Minister by the Brownists [in Amsterdam]."

[7]Wilson, "Another Look at John Canne," Church History, 34.

[8]Canne, A Necessitie of Separation, 2-3.

[9]Williams, Cottons Letter Examined, ed. Guild, Complete Writings, I, 381. See also pages 3886 and 393.

[10]John Canne, A Stay against Straying. Or an Answer to a Treatise, intituled: The Lawfulnes of hearing the ministers of the Church of England. By John Robinson. ([Amsterdam], 1639), 9-10.

[11]John Canne, A Voice from the Temple to the Higher Powers. Wherin is shewed, that it is the work and duty of saints, to search the prophecies and visions of holy Scripture, which concern the later times. (London, 1643), 1-10.

[12]John Ball, An Answer to Two Treatises of Mr. Iohn Can, the leader of the English Brownists in Amsterdam. The former called, A Necessitie of Separation from the Church of England . . . The other, A Stay against Straying . . . . (London, 1642), 87.

[13]E. B. Underhill, Records of a Church of Christ meeting in Broadmeed, Bristol, 1640-1687 (London, 1847).

[14]Jordan, Development of Religious Toleration, II, 224-25 and 251.

[15]Champlin Burrage, "Was John Canne A Baptist?" Transactions of the Baptist Historical Society (London, 1913), III, 212-46.

[16]Wilson, "John Canne," Church History, 38.

[17]See P. G. Rogers, The Fifth Monarchy Men (London, 1966), 92-92. A political as well as religious sect, the Fifth Monarchists anticipated the imminent arrival of the millennium and foresaw establishment of a theocratic regime of predestined saints who would impose discipline on the ungodly by force.

[18]A. S. P. Woodhouse, Puritanism and Liberty (London, 1938), 241-47.

[19]John Canne, A Voice from the Temple to the Higher Powers (London, 1653), 13-15 and 29.

[20]John Canne, et. al., A Narrative Wherein is faithfully set forth the Sufferings of John Canne, Wentworth Day, John Clarke . . . called, as their New Book saith, Fifth Monarchy Men, that is how eight of them were taken . . . as they were in the worship of God . . . and sent prisoners to the Counter. (London, 1658).

[21]D. B. Robertson, The Religious Foundations of Leveller Democracy (New York, 1951), 2 and 13.

[22]Haller, Liberty and Reformation, 216.

[23]Lilburne later called Rosier his "pastor and teacher." John Lilburne, The Legall Fundamentall Liberties of the People of England, revised, asserted, and vindicated. (London, 1649), 19 and 24.

[24]John Lilburne, The Resurrection of John Lilburne, now a prisoner in Dover-Castle, declared and manifested in these following lines penned by himself and now at his earnest desire published in print in these words (London, 1656), 7.

[25]John Lilburne, A Copie of a Letter . . . to Mr. William Prinne, Esq. (London, 1645), passim.

[26]Watts, 128.

[27]Canne, et. al., The Discoverer. Being an Answer to a Book entituled, Englands New Chain, the Second Part, Discovered (London, 1649), 56.

[28]Lilburne, Legall Fundamentall Liberties, 66; and George Thomason, Catalogue of the pamphlets, books, newspapers, and manuscripts relating to the civil war, the commonwealth, and restoration, collected by George Thomason, 1640-1661 (London, 1928), I, 214.

[29]Lilburne, Legall Fundamentall Liberties, 39 and 66; and Paget, A Defence of Chvrch-Government, 160.

[30]Robert Baillie, "Letter for Mr. D. D[ickson 23 July 12644]," The Letters and Journals of Robert Baillie A.M.: Principal of the University of Glasgow, ed. David Laing (Edinburgh, 1841-42), II, 212. Baillie was Professor of Divinity at Glasgow University who served as a Scottish delegate to the Westminster Assembly and was the primary leader of the Covenanter clergy.

[31]Gilpin, Millenarian Piety of Williams, 68.

[32]Forced to flee Massachusetts in 1638, Anne Hutchinson and her party of antinomians, including Clarke, purchased from the Indians the island of Aquidneck; on the northern end of the island they established the town of Portsmouth.

[33]Samuel G. Arnold, History of the State of Rhode Island and Providence Plantations (New York, 1859), I, 124.

[34]Thomas W. Bicknell, The Story of John Clarke (Providence, 1915), 101-03.

[35]Albert H. Newman, The New Schaff Herzog Religious Encyclopedia (Grand Rapids, Michigan, 1949-50), 127; The Dictionary of Religious Biography, 102; and H. Shelton Smith, Robert T. Handy, and Lefferts A. Loetscher, ed., American Christianity: An Historical Interpretation with Representative Documents (New York, 1960), 165-66.

[36]McLoughlin, New England Dissent, 11. In 1652 Clarke wrote that he was among those "who together for liberty of their consciences, and worship of their God, as their hearts were persuaded, long since fled from the persecuting hands of the Lordly Bishops" into the intolerance and persecution of Massachusetts. John Clarke, Ill Newes from New-England: or A Narative of New-Englands Persecution. Wherin is Declared that while old England is becoming new, New-England is become Old (London, 1652), in Collections of the Massachusetts Historical Society (1854), 4 ser., II, 34.

[37]Newman, Schaff herzog, 127.

[38]Winthrop, Journal, ed. Hosmer, I, 168.

[39]McLoughlin, New England Dissent, 11.

[40]Bynum Shaw, Divided We Stand (Durham, North Carolina, 1974), 45.

[41]Clarke, Ill Newes, passim. See also Roger Williams, "The copie of a letter of Roger Williams, of Providence, in New England, to Major Endicot, Governor of the Massachusetts, upon occasion of the late persecution against Mr. Clarke and Obadiah Holmes, and others, at Boston, the chief town of the Massachusetts in New England, August, 1651," ed. Bartlett, Complete Writings, VI, 214-18; and Williams, Bloody Tenent Yet More Bloody, ed. Caldwell, Complete Writings, IV, 524.

[42]Williams, "Letter of Williams to Endicot," ed. Bartlett, Complete Writings, VI, 214-28.

[43]Clarke, Ill Newes, 3, 11, 101, 52, and 99.

[44]Ibid., 20.

[45]Ibid., 106.

[46]Ibid., 15.

[47]Ibid., 108 and 104.

[48]Ibid., 100, 103, and 102.

[49]Ibid., 106.

[50]Clarke, Ill Newes, 12, 13, and 14.

[51]Watts, 92 and 213.

[52]Henry Vane, The Retired Man's Meditations; or, the Mysterie and Power of Godliness shining forth in the Living Word, to the unmasking the Mysterie of Iniquity in the Most refined and purest Forms . . . (London, 1655), passim, especially 322.

[53]Rogers, 134.

[54]Henry Vane, A healing Question propounded and resolved upon occasion of the late publique and seasonable call to humiliation, in order to love and union among the honest party . . . (London, 1656), 19.

[55]Henry Vane, A pilgrimage into the land of promise, by the light of the vision of Jacobs ladder and faith; or, a serious searched and prospect into life eternal . . . (n.p., 1664), 21-23.

[56]William Haller, Liberty and Reformation in the Puritan Revolution (New York, 1955), 1988-99.

[57]Thomas Edwards, Gangraena, or a Catalogue and Discovery of many of the Errors, Heresies, Blasphemies and pernicious practices of the Sectaries

of this time (London, 1646); John Saltmarsh, Groanes for Liberty: presented from the Presbyterian (formerly Non-conforming) brethren . . . in some treatises called Smectymnuus, to the high and hon. court of parliament in the Yeare 1641, by reason of prelates tyranny. (London, 1646), 44; and John Saltmarsh, Reasons for unitie, peace, and love (London, 1647), 7.

[58]John Saltmarsh, Sparkles of Glory, or Some Beams of the Morning-Star . . . to the establishment and pure enlargement of a Christian in Spirit and in Truth (London, 1647), 21-22, 116-21, 289-98, and 294-95. William Dell, Thomas Erbery, and Samuel Gorton held similar views.

[59]Ibid., 21-22. Regarding restoration of the true church, the seekers agreed with Williams, not Saltmarsh.

[60]Edwards, Gangraena, part III, 45.

[61]Watts, 185.

[62]William Braithwaite, The Beginnings of Quakerism; and Michael R. Watts, The Dissenters (Oxford, 1978), 185-85. If Braithwaite and Watts are correct this was in spite of the fact that George Fox had been attacked by John Jackson in Strength in Weakness, and responded to his criticisms and those of others in The Great Mistery of the Great Whore Unfolded: And Antichrists Kingdom Revealed unto Destruction (London, 1659), 217.

[63]J. F. McGregor, Radical Religion in the English Revolution (Oxford, 1984), 122.

[64]Saltmarsh, Sparkles of Glory, 289.

[65]Robert Baillie, Anabaptisme, the True Fountaine of Independency, Brownisme, Antinomy, Familisme and most of the other errours which for the time doe trouble the Church of England unsealed. (London, 1647), 96-97.

[66]McGregor contends that Jackson "sympathized rather than identified with the Seekers." McGregor, Radical Religion in the English Revolution, 123.

[67]John Jackson, A Sober Word to a Serious People (London, 1651), 32.

CHAPTER VI
THE PRINCIPLES OF SEPARATISM

Doctrinally, separatists and non-separatists held much in common. Both groups were rooted in the Calvinist tradition, both criticized the Anglican church for having failed to rid itself of the vestiges of Romanism, and both viewed prelacy as the primary barrier to reform. But the differences are even more striking. In this chapter, we will explore such ecclesiological issues as: the nature and definition of a true visible church; the origin and bases for gathered churches; limitations on ecclesiastical membership; grounds for discipline; the role and status of the Christian ministry; necessity of ecclesiastical supervision; autonomy for local congregations, reliance by churches on use of political force; and claims to apostolic succession.[1]

Even though there were doctrinal disagreements among the separatists, especially as the movement evolved over time, we can pinpoint certain fundamental ecclesiological and political principles accepted as axiomatic by all separatists. For the separatists a community does not need to be large to be an authentic sanctum sanctorum. A church is an independent, voluntary association of experiential believers with the right and power to meet and worship together, based on the pattern of the apostolic church. Matthew 18:20 ("where two or three are gathered") is the biblical base for such an understanding. For the separatists a church was only the size of one congregation, not a synod of many churches, and free of ecclesiastical supervision. The body of Christ consisted of many autonomous congregations rather than one unified, comprehensive institution. According to Robinson, a church is "a companie, consisting though but of two or three, separated from the world . . . and gathered into the name of Christ by a covenant." Smyth concurred: a worshipping community is "two, three or more saints joined together by covenant with God and themselves."[2] These definitions, based on a specific understanding of the Gospels and on the pattern of the earliest Christian churches, consist of several components to be discussed in the ensuing pages.

English separatism was distinguished by its doctrine of the militant, visible church which can be characterized by certain fundamental traits: a thoroughly reformed or pure church, a gathered ecclesia based on a voluntary covenant, church membership limited to a few designated saints, strict church discipline, congregational polity, absence of compulsion by the state, autonomy of the local group and rejection of ecclesiastical supervision, and opposition to established churches and to church-state systems. As set forth in the writings of Browne, Barrowe, Smyth, and Robinson, these are the sine qua non of separatism, except for the first which all puritans advocated.

A Pure Church

Among puritans, congregationalists, and separatists there was general agreement about the doctrinal teaching that holiness is of the essence of a properly constituted church of God. However, most presbyterians and non-separating congregationalists vehemently disagreed with the separatist declaration that the English church was not true because it refused renewal. For non-separatists the Roman Catholic Church was false because it failed to reform itself, but the Ecclesia Anglicana was not. For the separatists, on the other hand, the Anglican establishment had committed apostasy and was following antichrist. "We ought in no case to share our service betwixt Christ and anti-Christ," observed Robinson.[3] They decided that the Church of England and its ministry should be abandoned because it had not completely reformed itself and offered overlapping reasons for condemnation of the English church: corruption, failure to reform, lack of a covenantal base, admission of the unregenerate to membership (or lack of discipline), reliance on the power of the state rather than on voluntary participation, episcopacy instead of congregationalism, and absence of a legitimate claim to apostolic succession. One could desert English Christianity, according to these post-

Reformation dissidents, and still be a believer, since it was an impure, undisciplined church pervaded with "lamentable abuses, disorder and sins."[4]

A Voluntarily Gathered Church

For the separatists the biblical understanding of church government is grounded in neither ecclesiastical nor civil coercion. The visible society of God on earth dos not depend on compulsion, but exists wherever there is a group of the proven elect who have formed a collective covenant with God. So, a true church is a gathered, not an established, institution.[5] The separatists maintained that the church of Jesus Christ is a self-determined association of the regenerate (believers who have experienced the covenant of grace). They insisted on voluntary participation and believed that joining an ecclesia should be a free, uncoerced act of faith.[6] People should not be compelled to join against their will. "The Lordes kingdom is not by force, neither by an armie or strength, as be the kingdomes of this worlde," proclaimed Robert Browne in 1582. Based on that assumption, Browne contended that only a gathered church is scriptural. "The Church planted or gathered," he wrote, "is a companie or number of Christians or beleeuers, which by a willing couenant made with their God, are vnder the government of god and Christ, and kepe his laws in one holie communion."[7] Similarly, Barrowe condemned the Anglican authorities for "their false manner of seeking . . . to bring Christ in by the arme of flesh."[8] All separatists contended that an apostolic polity is not grounded in compulsion. The pure religious community is not dependent on force, but exists wherever there is a remnant of the regenerate who have formed a covenant with their Maker.[9] People are to be united voluntarily by a church covenant, not forced to attend worship services. Browne spoke of members of a pure congregation being bound together "by a willing covenant made with their God." Unlike Williams, who relied primarily on New Testament exegesis, Browne justified his position with the Old Testament examples of Moses and the Israelites having formed "a couenant to seeke the Lord God of their fathers."[10]

Because the Tudor-Stuart Church lacked a covenantal base, it was by separatist standards inappropriately constituted--hence illegitimate. England had become Protestant by governmental decree, rather than by public consent. Commenting on this in 1592 Barrowe penned, "All this people, with all these manners [of sin], were in one daye, with the blast of Queen Elizabeth's trumpet, of ignorance papistes and grosse idolaters, made faithful Christianes, and true professors [by the Act of Uniformity of 1559]."[11] Robinson later added:

> In the forming of your [Richard Bernard's] national English Church by a new covenant from that wherein it stood in Popery, which was . . . I add with Antichrist in the stead of Christ, no such profession of faith was made, as yourself do both require and prove necessary for the forming of the visible church.[12]

Robinson acknowledged that Anglicanism was in accord with much of Christian teaching, but he contended that doctrine alone does not make a church authentic. It must be grounded in a covenant and include only the elect. "We admit," he wrote, "the ministers of England taught soundly in all the points of religion . . . yet this did no way prove them true ministers of Christ."[13] Smyth concurred that "the constitution of the Anglican Church is a false constitution because it lacks a covenant."[14] The Ecclesia Anglicana was an established, not a gathered, church since it was not based on voluntarism. Non-believers, as well as believers, were members. Insofar as the official church relied on the power of government, it was corrupt and false.

Reform Led by Saints

For most puritans the only important distinction between people is whether they have been reborn spiritually. But the separatist ideal went a step beyond puritan orthodoxy in the intensity of the perfectionistic search for a disciplined and pure society of Jesus Christ. Browne wrote that "he judged that the kingdom of God was not to be begun by whole parishes, but rather off the worthiest, were thei neuer so feuve."[15] The separatists believed they were God's elect--His visible saints--chosen to lead the way to reformation "without tarying for anie." They rejected the Calvinist teaching that reform would be carried out through state action, contending instead that those who see the need should bring about change.

Believing that membership should be restricted to the worthiest, separatists sought exclusion of the reprobate. As John Robinson taught they "must sever and select the good from the evil."[16] Accordingly, for a church to be properly constituted, it should not consist of every citizen in a nation, not even of all those who have been baptized; rather it should be composed only of visible saints: Christians able to provide evidence of saving faith.[17] Barrowe declared, "What a preposterous dealing is this, to receave the wicked unto the Lordes table."[18] The militant apostolic church, Robinson insisted two decades later, did not mix the faithful with the unregenerate, but admitted only the former: "Jesus and his apostles appointed none other true visible churches but particular congregations of faithful people."[19] Insofar as they allowed only the regenerate to join and excluded others, they were exclusive, closed communities. Williams agreed with the early separatists that only a few would be saved, but condemned persecution of the reprobate.

The first separatists believed that in order to avoid personal sin it was the duty of real Christians to separate form the corruption, impurity, and impropriety of both the established church and the world. Robinson taught that "by abetting sin and corruption a church enwraps herself in the same guilt with the sinner . . . and ceaseth to be any longer the true church of Christ."[20] As their principal authority, separatists pointed to II Corinthians 6:17, "Come ye out from among them and separate yourselves, saith the Lord." In A Justification of Separation Robinson queried rhetorically, "What statute or canon was there, that the Corinthians should suffer amongst them the incestuous person unreformed? And yet for so doing this 'little leaven leavens the whole lump'?"[21] Obviously, Robinson thought such an "incestuous person" should be excluded form communion with the faithful, in accord with the Corinthian example.[22]

The separatists contended that the Church of England lacked discipline and was not adequately selective in its membership requirements, since it allowed everyone born within the nation who was baptized to become a Christian. "None are here refused, none kept out," wrote Barrowe, "[The Anglican Church does not deny] . . . baptisme to even whores and witches; she receaveth them al into her coueanant (which is not with God, but with death and hell)."[23] For this reason Barrowe favored separation, stating: "Because al the profane and wicked of the lande are received into the bodie of your church."[24] According to the separatists, the Anglican church was corrupt because it allowed anyone to join, permitted the reprobate to commune with the elect, and maintained a promiscuous membership.[25]

Because the official church was not a reformed body, they felt it should be repudiated.

Discipline Locally Administered

To maintain a rightly constituted church, rigorous internal discipline is required which calls for adherence to true Christian conduct. Organization necessitates control, so ecclesiastical discipline was essential to the separatists. Greater demands were placed on members of separated communities than on those connected with the official church. Separatists believed that discipline is the primary mark of the true worshipping community, although right belief and sacraments were also essential. Through provincial ecclesiastical control they sought to insure purity among the flock. Responsibility for ecclesiastical discipline lies with the local congregation; standard of membership should be determined and enforced locally. Only the local church has the right to determine or control membership national officials, courts, and organizations lack such a prerogative. Comparing the role of a pastor with that of a father, Robinson asked rhetorically, "Doth any law, either Divine or human, deny a father liberty to correct his own children?"[26] He and the other separatists believed central discipline and control to be unnecessary. The jurisdiction of national authorities, the monarch included, should be severely limited.

Browne said that "the Lords people is of the willing sorte," indicating opposition to compulsion in religious affairs.[27] He believed that ministers should not rely on governmental authority to enforce the faith. Clergy, rather than civic officials, should discipline the flocks. Browne contended that

> there is no ende of their pride and crueltie, which ascende vp and sit in the Magistrates chaire and smite the people with a continuall plague, and such of them as haue not yet gotten the roume, do crie for Discipline, Discipline, that is, for a ciuill forcing to imprison the people. But the Lorde shall bring them downe to the dust and to the pitt, as abhominable carkasses.[28]

The separatists believed that ecclesiastical reform was the responsibility of the clergy and saints, not of government officials. To do otherwise is to give the secular authorities more influence in church affairs than Christ. Are not, Browne asked, those who tarry for a ruler "ashamed thus to slander the Magistrate" by waiting for official government action? "For the spiritual power of Christ and his Church, and the Keys of binding and loosing, they take from Christ and give to the Magistrate."[29]

The queen may, Browne asserted, brandish the sword in temporal concerns. She may even "put to death all that deserve it by law, either of the Church or commonwealth, and none may resist her . . . by force or by wicked speeches," But, she lacks that right to "copell [compel] religion, to plant Churches by power, and to force a submission to Ecclesiastical gouernement."[30] To force people to believe is to "usurp the throne of Jesus Christ."[31] The church need not depend on the police power of the state. Indeed, the church often has flourished during times of persecution. "For we knowe that when Magistrates haue bin most of all against the Church and the authorities thereof, the Church hath most florished."[32]

Browne's position on church and state seems ambiguous, having varied throughout his life. Originally Browne was willing to accept governmental-sponsored reform.

> Browne had no intention [according to Burrage] of instituting any permanent separation of all churches from one another. The idea of a State Church doubtless seemed to him as desirable as to any other English citizen. He would undoubtedly have used the Parish church buildings, practically as they stood, for his congregational churches.[33]

For most of his adult life Browne was an erastian congregationalist. Unlike Williams, during both the pre- and post-separatist phases of his intellectual development, he accepted the idea of a state church. He believed that government officials should enforce the true religion. Even during his brief separatist phase he had erastian tendencies, in spite of his disillusionment with the halfway reformation of the Elizabethan religious settlement.[34] When the queen refused to support a thorough reform, Browne chose to separate--all the while proclaiming his loyalty and the provisional nature of his actions. Most of his life he accepted political intervention in the life of the church, even when he declared that the ecclesia must not await governmental action to bring about reform.

While Browne believed that royal authority should be circumscribed and not employed "to copell [compel] religion," it could be employed as "a means of keeping the churches under state control and so of ensuring in them a reasonable amount of unity in belief and practice." "Our magistrates," he said, "[may] reform the church and command things expedient for the same" just as Moses reformed the faith of Israel.[35]

Though Browne contemplated an absolute monarchy,his innovative notions abetted the trend toward ecclesiastical democracy or self-government. Browne taught an indwelling Christ. His doctrine of the church was of a spiritual monarchy ruled by Jesus as Lord. He advocated Christocracy, not democracy. However, because Jesus was invisible, his will was not always discernible. Thus, lay participation in decision-making emerged within subsequent generations of separatist communities, in part because of different interpretations of the divine will. Browne was aware that dissension might erupt since believers had different understandings, but he was confident that the magistrates would be able to curb it. In a letter written in 1588 during his post-separatist phase, Browne declared "that the Civil Magistrate must restraine that licentiousness" of "all factions and heresies."[36]

Rejection of Ecclesiastical Supervision

The separatists perceived prelacy as a major obstacle to reform. Suspicious of authority, they wanted a church without bishops, synods, vestments, or altars. In A Just and Necessarie Apologie Robinson declared that there is no need for supervisors: "Two or three or more people making Peter's confession, Matthew 26:16, are the church even though they may make this confession without officers." He further stated that "the bishops and other ecclesiastical leaders have no basis in scripture. Scripture speaks only of apostles, prophets, evangelists, pastors, and teachers." Most English separatists, except Browne, wanted an ecclesia governed by laymen and by clergy elected by the congregation. They contended that the New Testament pattern of organization was non-bureaucratic. There were, in Robinson's words, no "Grand Metropolitans, archbishops, bishops, suffragans, deans, archdeacons, chancellors, officials, and the residue of that lordly clergy" in the earliest church.[37] The government's indictment against Barrowe and Greenwood declared "that they disallowed the aucthoritie of bishops."[38] Nor in the view of Smyth is presbyterianism legitimate: "The eldership is the invention of man."[39] Robinson noted "there is no king of the church but Christ."[40] For these spiritual revolutionaries the ecclesial hierarchy was responsible for the corruption of Anglicanism. Browne called the bishops "puddle water" compared with Christ. During an interrogation by the prelacy, Barrowe scoffed that "your church is not governed by Christe's Testament, but by the Romish courtes and canons, etc."[41] Several decades later Williams wrote, "All the grounds and principles leading to oppose Bishops, Ceremonies, and Common Prayer doe necessarily . . . conclude a separation of holy from unholy."[42]

Williston Walker once wrote that "congregationalism has always accorded large liberty to local churches in their interpretation of doctrine and polity."[43] By the 1640s, if not before, even John Cotton believed in the doctrine of a gathered church in the relative independence of each congregation. In 1644 in The Keyes of the Kingdom of Heaven Cotton asserted that the individual congregation is the basic unit of the Christian church: "The complete integrity of a minister's calling" lies with the power the people in his congregation give to him.[44] Yet, in the same work Cotton highlighted the necessity of communion among the churches not only through synods but by receiving the Lord's Supper in sister churches. While all congregations are equal and independent, any of the them can be admonished, and if necessary condemned, by a synod or other ecclesiastical means. (See, for example, Cotton's 1643 tract, The Doctrine of the Church, To which is committed the Keyes of the Kingdome of Heaven.)[45] Unlike separatism, seventeenth-century congregationalism did not oppose hierarchical structures.

Contrary to Williams, but like Cotton, Browne did not advocate complete independence for each congregation, but taught that churches should be connected loosely.[46] Fellowship with other bodies of saints was a duty and privilege. A company having difficulty determining the will of God should seek advice from other congregations as a group, not as individuals. Browne was not an isolationist. He defended the use of "synods or meetings of sundry churches" in situations in which "the weaker churches seeke helpe of the stronger."[47] Synods are to be encouraged insofar as their status is advisory, but no church is to have authority over another. Moreover, a synod was to be composed of the churches themselves, not of representatives. Williams later disagreed; he was skeptical about the propriety of synods.

Condemnation of the Ecclesia Anglicana and of All Other Church-State Establishments

Distinguishing between non-separatists and separatists, Perry Miller refers to "those who called everything about the Church corrupt" and to "those who called the Church itself corrupt."[48] By separatist standards, the Church of England was not a true Christian church. Having been corrupted, what passed as the religious institution founded by Jesus Christ had ceased completely to be a body of Christ. Williams contended that English Christianity was working in cooperation with Antichrist. In this regard Barrowe wrote:

> Neither can I see how anie can anie longer mistake that adulterous Church of England that sitteth upon all the confused people as vpon manie waters. We are so far from honoring her with the title of a church.

> There is no comparison betweene these holy churches of God, which were truly gathered and these their confused idolatrous assemblies. They in nothing can be compared unto these churches, but in sinne and error.[49]

"With what conscience can any man plead the saintship of all that godless crew in the English assemblies?" queried Robinson in 1610. "Without the due observations of which rules [in Christ's Testament], they can have no true ministerie, sacraments, exercises, communion, gospel."[50] The primary reason the English church was improperly constituted was because it contained unconverted people, therefore its polity, its exercise of discipline, its liturgy, and its sacraments were unapostolic.

The Anglican claim to apostolic succession (a commission derived only from Christ and the apostles) is thus false. With the rise of the papacy in the late Roman world, authentic churches ceased to exist. Separatists denied the Stuart claim to apostleship primarily because it differed from that of Christ; neither the English church nor any extant ecclesiastical system is in accord with the apostolic archetype. Robinson asserted that Christ and his disciples "did not by the co-active laws of men shuffle together good and bad, as intending a new monster or chimera, but admitted of such, and none other, as confessed their sin and justified God."[51] Implicitly, the separatists were saying that there was no salvation through the Anglican church. Anticlericalism is inherent in such a notion. The separatist belief that grace did not come to believers through the Anglican ministry was a fundamental attack on the established system of ordaining clergy.

The advocates of "reformation without tarrying" denied episcopal or presbyterial jurisdiction over believers. Greenwood wrote, "We are throughe the same spirit and worde of trueth delivered from all subjection of antichrist, of the false church, false ministerie, false government, etc."[52] Robinson contended that the church which "enwraps herself in the same guilt with the sinner . . . ceaseth to be any longer the true church of Christ."[53] Barrowe rejected the Anglican "assemblies to be the true churches of Christ." Robinson added, "We dare no dip in their meal [in the official communion services] lest we be soured by their leaven." Browne had made a similar comment in 1582, "Know yet not (saith the scripture) that a little leaven leaventh the whole lump."[54] Robinson justified severing relations with the official church, saying that "we ought to communicate both in prayer, and in all the other ordinances of God, with all God's children, except they themselves hinder it, or put a bar which we are persuaded they in the Church of England do."[55] If the Anglican church was untrue, then its worship, its ecclesiastical hierarchy, and its sacraments were impure also, and true believers were justified in separating from it.

Robinson, like Williams, denied that any contemporary church was genuine. "No church in the world now hath," Robinson taught, "that absolute promise of the Lord's visible presence, which that church the Jewish Church then had, till the coming of Christ."[56] However, whereas Robinson and the early separatists reserved their invective to the Anglican church, Williams and several separatists who lived during the Interregnum denounced all existing churches and their ministries. Eventually, he minimized the distinction between laity and clergy and denied that any existing church was a real Christian community.

Not only did the most forward of the separatists refuse to admit other Christians to their congregations, they often did not consent to prayer, fellowship, or take eucharistic communion with members of the Church of

England.[57] Cartwright wrote that the main difference between Harrison and himself was "the receaving without publique repentaunce of those which come from the Churches of England."[58] Smyth agreed with Bernard's assertion that the separatists believed that "it's not lawful to hear any ministers"of the English Church. And Robinson professed in 1610, "We may not communicate at all in that ministry, which is exercised by an unlawful person or in an unlawful place . . . lest we do evil."[59] But Williams and Canne were more radical than earlier generations of English sectarians. Whereas Robinson and others maintained that it was sinful to join in prayer or sharing of the sacraments with Anglicans, Williams adamantly insisted that it was wrong to join in any act of worship, including preaching, oaths and prayer, with the unconverted; even to attend an Anglican worship service was to be condemned.

In conclusion, in the process of challenging England's episcopal system, the English separatists instituted a new church polity based on the principle of ecclesiastical self-government. Their biblically-based theology, especially the ecclesiology, had profound implications for church and social history and played a significant role in the subsequent multiplication of denominations and sects. Specifically the separatist concept of a gathered church deviated substantially from the norm, placing them at the forefront of the free church movement that grew out of Tudor puritanism. The separatists were among the few willing to risk forming religious institutions outside the jurisdiction of accepted practice. They were a critical element in the development of a congregational form of church organization and voluntaristic doctrines. The separatists were primarily preachers who advocated unusual views; through the impact of their ideas they contributed to the growth of a democratic theory of church government and possibly indirectly to the development of modern social thought.

As sectarians, the English separatists were harbingers of modern denominationalism. Their doctrines and practices gave Christianity a significant impetus toward diversity, assisting in the transformation from a religiously uniform to a pluralistic society. Prior to their liberation in the new land, the separatists and other underground religious communities were treated as illicit sects. The seeds of sectarianism initially failed to take root in England because of the hostile caesaro-papistic environment, yet when replanted in the American soil separatism and its baptist offshoots flourished. In the colonies, in time, separatist thought was able to grow and differentiate, though in the process it contributed toward the splintering of Christianity. Today we are all, in one sense, separated brethren. The pattern of ecclesiastical organization developed in separated churches was one important model for future generations of religious people and organizations.

Chapter 6

Endnotes

[1]Although the primary concern is with the mature thought of each thinker and how those ideas relate to the world view of Roger Williams, the theology of each separatist changed over time as they went through various stages of development along the continuum that led from religious separation to separatism of church and state.

[2]Robinson, Of Religious Communion, ed. Ashton, Works, II, 132; and Smyth, Principles and Inferences, ed. Whitley, Works, I, 258.

Browne defined a church as a "companie or number of Christian beleeuers." Robert Browne, A Booke Which Sheweth the Life and Manners of All Trve Christians, and howe vnlike they are vnto Turkes and Papistes, and Heathen folke (Middelburg, 1582), ed. Peel and Carlson, Writings of Harrison and Browne, 253.

[3]Robinson, A Justification of Separation, ed. Ashton, Works, II, 54.

[4]Browne, Trve and Short Declaration, ed. Peel and Carlson, Writings of Harrison and Browne, 399.

[5]True is a favorite word of the separatists; when applied to a church, it generally referred to a pure, uncorrupted, reformed, and biblical ecclesiastical institution which was constituted in accord with the apostolic tradition.

[6]Browne, Booke Which Sheweth, ed. Peel and Carlson, Writings, 227 and 253-57; Robinson, A Justification of Separation, ed. Ashton, Works, II, 9-10; and Smyth, Works, I, 258-59.

According to separatist thinking, the church does not depend on position, power, edicts, force, or establishments. Nor is it determined by geographical, political, or national categories, divisions, or areas. For this reason, separatists spoke of the gathered church as an institution established by a group of Christians on the basis of a covenant. They believed the pure community was one which had been voluntarily assembled, not institutionally determined. By the 1640s even John Cotton believed in the doctrine of a gathered church.

[7]Browne, Reformation without Tarying, ed. Peel and Carlson, Writings, I, 161-62; and Browne, A Booke Which sheweth, ed. Peel and Carlson, Writings of Harrison and Browne, 253.

[8]Barrowe, Briefe Discoverie, ed. Carlson, Writings, 1587-90, III, 557.

[9]A true visible church originates, the separatists declared, with a voluntary covenant among a group of Christian saints with God. It does not depend on compulsion, but exists wherever a band of two or more can be found who have truly experienced rebirth and are professed believers.

[10]Browne, Booke Which Sheweth, ed. Peel and Carlson, Writings, I, 253; and Browne, Reformation without Tarying, ed. Peel and Carlson, Writings, I, 163.

[11]Barrowe, Briefe Discoverie, ed. Carlson, Writings, 1587-90, III, 283.

[12]Robinson, A Justification of Separation, ed. Ashton, Works, II, 399.

[13]Ibid., 388.

[14]John Smyth, Paralleles, Censvres, Observations (Amsterdam, 1609), ed. Whitley, Works of John Smyth, II, 339.

[15]Browne, Trve and Short Declaration, ed. Peel and Carlson, Writings of Harrison and Browne, 404.

[16]Robinson, A Just and Necessarie Apologie, ed. Ashton, Works, II, 14. The presbyterians also believed in exclusion of those reprobate who can be clearly identified through acts of sinning. However, they sought exclusion on procedural or empirical not theological grounds; people in the congregation were allowed to remain members unless specifically excommunicated. Whereas separatists possessed a high definition of membership, presbyterians had a low definition and congregationalists a moderate understanding.

[17]Browne, Reformation without Tarying, ed. Peel and Carlson, Writings, I, 156.

[18]Barrowe, Briefe Discoverie, ed. Carlson, Writings, 1587-90, III, 318.

[19]Robinson, A Just and Necessarie Apologie, ed. Ashton, Works, III, 332.

[20]Robinson, Of Religious Communion, ed. Ashton, Works, II, 260.

[21]Robinson, A Just and Necessarie Apologie, ed. Ashton, Works, III, 21.

[22]Anglican authorities, like most seventeenth-century Protestants, believed every person born within their nation, once baptized, was automatically a Christian. The presumption was that all citizens should be considered members of Christ's church, regardless of the quality of their spiritual lives or ability to prove election. Separatists disagreed; they were convinced that all national churches, especially the English church, lacked selectivity in requirements for membership.

[23]Barrowe, Briefe Discoverie, ed. Carlson, Writings, 1587-90, III, 281.

[24]Henry Barrow, "Barrow's Fourth Examination, March 18, 1588," ed. Carlson, Writings, 1587-90, III, 179.

[25]Robinson wrote derogatorily,, "The Church of England is not a very beautiful bird. . . .It consists of a mixture of Egyptian bondage, Babylonish

confusion, carnal pomp, and a company of Jewish, heathenish, and popish ceremonies." Robinson, A Justification of Separation, ed. Ashton, Works, I, 59.

[26]Robinson, A Just and Necessarie Apologie, ed. Ashton, Works, III, 11.

[27]Browne, Reformation without Tarying, ed. Peel and Carlson, Writings of Harrison and Browne, 162.

[28]Ibid.

[29]Ibid., 152-53.

[30]Browne, Reformation without Tarying, ed. Peel and Carlson, Writings of Harrison and Browne, 152 and 164.

[31]Browne, Booke which Sheweth, ed. Peel and Carlson, Writings of Harrison and Browne, 330.

[32]Browne, Reformation without Tarying, ed. Peel and Carlson, Writings of Harrison and Browne, 168.

[33]Burrage, Early English Dissenters, 103-04.

[34]Frederick Powicke was the first scholar to call Browne an erastian congregationalist in Robert Browne, 79. See Browne, Reformation without Tarying, ed. Peel and Carlson, Writings of Harrison and Browne, 167.

[35]Browne, Reformation without Tarying, ed. Peel and Carlson, Writings of Harrison and Browne, 164.

[36]Robert Browne, A "New Years Guift": An Hitherto Lost Treatise by Robert Browne, the Father of Congregationalism. In the form of a Letter to his uncle Mr. Flowers (December 31, 1588). ed. Champlin Burrage (London, 1924), 30.

[37]Robinson, Just and Necessarie Apologie, ed. Ashton, Works, III, 133, 171, and 171.

[38]Barrowe and Greenwood, "The Arraig[n]ment of Certaine Puritanes or Brownists the Second of Aprill, 1593," ed. Carlson, Writings of Greenwood and Barrow, VI, 273.

[39]John Smyth, Differences of the Churches of the Separation: Contayning, a Description of the Leitovrgie and Ministerie of the Visible Church (Amsterdam, 1608), ed. Whitley, Works of John Smyth, I, 297.

[40]Robinson, A Justification of Separation, ed. Ashton, Works, II, 31.

[41]Browne, Reformation without Tarying, ed. Peel and Carlson, Writings, I, 153; and Barrowe, "Fourth Examination," ed. Carlson, Writings, 1587-90, III, 179.

[42]Williams, Cottons Letter Examined, ed. Guild, Complete Writings, I, 109.

[43]Williston Walker, The Creeds and Platforms of Congregationalism (New York, 1893), xv.

[44]Cotton, Keyes of the Kingdom, 37.

[45]John Cotton, The Doctrine of the Church, To which is committed the Keyes of the Kingdome of Heaven (Boston, 1643), passim.

[46]Browne, Booke Which Sheweth, ed. Peel and Carlson, Writings of Harrison and Browne, 222-395.

[47]Browne, Trve and Short Declaration, ed. Peel and Carlson, Writings of Harrison and Browne, 420.

[48]Miller, Orthodoxy in Massachusetts, 71.

[49]Barrowe, Briefe Discoverie, ed. Carlson, Writings, 1587-90, III, 595 and 304.

[50]Robinson, A Justification of Separation, ed. Ashton, Works, II, 260; and Barrowe, Briefe Discoverie, ed. Carlson, Writings, 1587-90, III, 570.

[51]Robinson, A Just and Necessarie Apologie, ed. Ashton, Works, III, 114.

[52]Greenwood, An Answere to George Gifford's Pretended Defence of Read Praiers and Devised Litourgies, ed. Carlson, Writings of Greenwood, IV, 91.

[53]Robinson, A Justification of Separation, ed. Ashton, Works, II, 259.

[54]Barrowe, Briefe Discoverie, ed. Carlson, Writings, 1587-90, III, 308; Robinson, A Just and Necessarie Apologie, ed. Ashton, Works, III, 15; and Browne, Reformation without Tarying, ed. Peel and Carlson, Writings, I, 169.

[55]Robinson, A Justification of Separation, ed. Ashton, Works, II, 260.

[56]Ibid., II, 463-64.

[57]Ibid., II, 15, 24, and 463. There were some differences among separatists as to their attitudes towards maintaining relations with Anglicans. Robinson was somewhat more tolerant concerning contact than all except Smyth, but even he shunned those whom he felt were corrupt.

[58]Thomas Cartwright, <u>An Answere vnto a Letter of Master Harrisons by Master Cartwright being at Middelborough</u> (Middelburg, [1585]), ed. Albert Peel and Leland H. Carlson, <u>Cartwrightiana</u> (London, 1951), 52.

[59]Smyth, <u>Paralleles, Censvres</u>, ed. Whitley, <u>Works</u>, II, 337; and Robinson, <u>A Justification of Separation</u>, ed. Ashton, <u>Works</u>, II, 16.

CHAPTER VII

WILLIAMS WITHIN THE CONTEXT OF SEPARATISM

There were many points of similarity between Roger Williams's beliefs and those of his predecessors. In one sense, his "newe and dangerous opinions" of liberty and separation resembled scores of others; differences were primarily a matter of degree. But it is of utmost importance to realize that his beliefs were distinctive, even though they were built upon a foundation of five decades of separatist tradition. The conclusions Williams drew from principles promulgated by the first and second generation of separatists went further than his precursors ever imagined possible; his doctrine of separation of church and state was revolutionary in its degree of subversion.

The contrast between Roger Williams and the original separatists is often stark. The Brownists, Barrowists, and Pilgrims were besieged minorities constantly on the defensive against the powers and principalities of the world. By their commitment and actions, the first separatists accomplished much, embarking successfully on a path that challenged the vestiges of the past. Yet, circumstances had pushed them unwillingly to separate; because they were unable to convert the monarch to puritanism, they were compelled to break with the official church. They discovered a novel form of church organization, but did not grasp the philosophical justification for alternative definitions of the roles of church and government. They were concerned with certain, specific, religious grievances and with their own right to worship, not with the freedom of other unusual agitators. In sum, they had no intention of reconstructing the social order, only of denying the power of the bishops and in purifying their own congregations.

Williams, though, took the offensive against all church-state establishments by promulgating a new vision and developing a revolutionary, thorough counterproposal to erastianism. Williams argued with more consistency and in a more comprehensive manner than his predecessors. He sought to avoid the ambiguities in Calvinist and separatist thought. Williams conceived a fresh understanding of the origin, nature, role, and purpose of the body politic. For him the modern state is a secular, utilitarian institution based on a non-religious covenant; thus, it lacks any divine role or significance. Government exists independent of the convictions of its citizenry and of church dogma and constraint. The office of magistrate is "merely and essentially Civill."[1] Williams contributed, as this suggests, to the development of the modern concept of the impartial, secular state--an institution which allows for religious freedom and choice--by moving separatism intellectually from a preoccupation with personal freedom and faith to espousal of broad-based political principles.

> The civil state [Williams contended] is humbly to be implored, to provide in their high Wisdome for the security of all the respective consciences, in their respective meetings and the beauty of civility and humanity be maintained among the chiefe opposers and dissenters.[2]

Frequently, the early separatists thought matters through only after having acted already. Doctrine usually succeeded practice for them. Preoccupied with the strategy of the moment, and lacking an historical model, they were unable to conceptualize the broad implications of their nonconforming ideas and actions. Although the first separatists were willing to face ostracism and even death for their beliefs, they never realized the full import of their views. Separateness was an indeterminate concept, clarified over several decades. History is a process. The early separatists conceived of something radical for their time--yet moderate compared with the ideas of later generations of separatists. Williams's views were a logical step in a process that evolved over time.

From the outset, the Brownists and Barrowists, but not the Pilgrims, faced a dilemma in that they adhered to magisterial control over the church while concurrently acknowledging being subject to Christ only. Unlike Williams, who cut the Gordian knot by disavowing magisterial supremacy, they continued to seek government-enforced religious uniformity. The early separatists did not have the vision to develop a comprehensive or coherent plan for a congregationally-based ecclesiastical or political structure. While they dissociated themselves and their congregations from that which they believed to be false, none of the pioneers arrived at the far-reaching, positive principle of complete independence between the society of God and that of the world. As a persecuted sect, the original separatists were compelled by the circumstances to be concerned with personal liberty. Consequently, theirs was a negative doctrine of withdrawal focused on individual and congregational concerns, not the more abstract principle of toleration. Under the pressures of the moment, they obtained religious liberty for themselves by disassociating from the corruption of a particular state-controlled church, the Church of England, not from all state churches.

Williams must be distinguished from Robert Browne, Henry Barrowe, and John Calvin on this point. Williams advanced separatism ideologically by espousing a clearly formulated and unequivocal principle of separation. The separation Williams urged was different; it was more universal. Williams advocated a complete independence of the spiritual and natural worlds, rather than withdrawal from only one specific church. In all probability, Calvin would have rejected Williams's reasoning in this regard.[3] Only the se-baptist John Smyth approached Williams's doctrine of freedom for all believers to practice their faith without government interference. For people today Williams's principle seems implicit in the earlier axiom, but for the seventeenth century such connections were not so obvious. Unlike Williams, the Elizabethan secessionists were uanware of the corollary principle that the state should be free from ecclesiastical control. Williams's forerunners never spoke on behalf of government freedom from the influence of the clergy. The first separatists rebelled against the English system, hence to some extent against Reformed ecclesiology and political theory, but the implications were made obvious only by Williams's willingness to pursue separateness to the point of separation as the ultimate logical conclusion. Williams differed from his predecessors in that by the 1640s he rejected orthodox Calvinistic understandings of church-state relations. Williams had taken a major intellectual leap in contrast even with his contemporaries, as witnessed by the millenarian views of John Canne and others like him who continued to adhere to the earlier position and specifically rejected Williams's doctrine of civil liberty. Though a separatist throughout his life, Canne rejected separation of church and state, believing instead that the government has the right to support the true church with all the power at its command. As a Fifth Monarchist, he was committed to rule by the elect.

Carrying the Reformed doctrine of election to a logical outcome, Tudor separatists believed that they and their groups would be saved regardless of merit. In A Paterne of True Prayer written in 1605, even John Smyth initially affirmed his belief in the Calvinist doctrine of predestination.[4] However, by the time Smyth wrote his confession of faith in Propositions and Conclusions (1610) he rejected double predestinatio and tended toward Arminianism. Smyth declared, instead, that Christ died for everyone, though only the faithful benefit.[5] Browne, Barrowe, and Robinson opposed compulsory church attendance and attacked the policy of admitting everyone to an all-inclusive national church. Their ecclesiology was more exclusive than Williams's. They saw no place for unbelievers in an authentic Christian company.[6] Thus, the corollary concept of a covenant became the foundation for their ecclesiology.

Although Calvin always had been careful to acknowledge that only God knows who is among the invisible elect, while simultaneously insisting that certain individuals have been predestined for salvation since the beginning of time, in practice Calvin acted as if he were such a person. Seemingly unaware of Calvin's caveat, the Tudor separatists viewed themselves as having been specially chosen.[7] In contrast, despite many subtle indications that he considered himself a witness or prophet crying in the wilderness, Williams was skeptical that anyone (other than possibly himself) was among the elect. On several occasions Williams declared that there are no chosen communities or nations, but he seldom if ever commented on the salvation of any particular individual.[8] The feeling that he conveyed was that nearly everyone is eternally doomed. Clearly for him there were (at that time) no true churches, no authentic ministers, and probably few, if any, legitimate saints. He denied that any contemporary nation or church can legitimately claim to be chosen by God. Williams believed that no congregation will possess divine sanction until the advent of the millennium.

While it may not have been Browne's initial desire, congregationalism became a measure of separatism. The separatists believed that the biblical teaching about church polity was congregational, a thought which Williams accepted as axiomatic prior to emigrating to America. Subsequently, Williams focused less on purely ecclesiastical concerns and more on individual and political considerations. Initially, Smyth described the church as a body composed of "saincts" formed by "a covenant."[9] For Barrowe discipline was more important than the sacraments in characterizing an ecclesia.[10] Through a covenant, discipline was to be imposed. Implicit within all of these understandings is the supposition that there are many separate congregations rather than merely one unified Christian church.

Characteristically, Williams carried this a step further by defining the church vis-a-vis other organizations within society. Churches are at best private voluntary associations which resemble all other social institutions within a community. From this point of view, religious bodies lose their special status and prerogatives. While guaranteed basic civil rights, they are no longer accorded singular deference. Religious associations are fundamentally no different from other private institutions in the manner in which they are treated by law and government. Inherent within Williams's definition is the assumption that even though churches may possess special understandings of spirituality, their social status is no greater than that of any other private association. Belonging to a church is no different from membership in a labor union, political party, social club, or charitable organization.

Williams's accent on independence is demonstrated by his resolute reaction to participation in English worship services. John Robinson decided, twenty years before Williams arrived in Massachusetts, that his followers could attend the Anglican services without being tainted so long as they did not partake of the sacraments. Williams condemned such actions as sinful, and Smyth, Canne, and Clarke concurred with him. Not only did the most forward of the separatists refuse to admit non-separatists to their congregation, they often refused to pray or have fellowship with parishioners of the official national church, implicitly denying that any Anglican could be among the hidden elect.[11] Smyth, for instance, agreed with Bernard's assertion that separatists held that "it's not lawful to hear any ministers" of the English Church."[12] And Robinson professed in 1610, "We may not communicate at all in that ministry, which is exercised by an unlawful person or in an unlawful place . . . lest we do evil."[13] But Roger Williams was more radical than his precursors. Whereas Robinson maintained that it was wrong to join in prayer or to partake in the eucharist with an Anglican, Williams adamantly insisted that it was sinful to participate with the unconverted in any form of worship--prayer, communion, singing, and oaths. A believer who attends a worship service conducted by an Anglican priest should be excommunicated by the Massachusetts churches. Hence, soon after arriving in the Bay colony, Williams demanded that the Bostonians repent for having ever participated in Anglican services. Initially, that demand was the primary issue which divided Williams from the leadership in Massachusetts and tipped them off as to his revolutionary spirit.

Williams's intellectual journey most closely resembled that of Smyth, who likewise progressed from puritanism to separatism to believers' baptism, although Williams (after banishment) may have moved a step further to seekerism. Yet there were differences. After deciding that self-baptism was fallacious, Smyth concluded that a true church did exist on earth: the Mennonite Church he discovered in the Netherlands. On the other hand, Williams (like Robinson) denied that any contemporary religious community was legitimate. Convinced that there would be no true churchly institutions until God raisers new prophets, by the 1640s Williams refused to participate in any official church at all.[14]

In the eyes of the Elizabethan and Jacobean separatists, ascendancy of the papacy during the early middle ages had resulted in the extinction of all true churches. Barrowe declared "there is not a true church in England."[15] Smyth professed that the faith, government, ministry, and worship of the Church of England was unbiblical and thus false.[16] Williams concurred, as demonstrated by his conflict with the leadership in Massachusetts over attending English worship services. Since Williams taught that it is necessary to separate from such false religious communities before uniting with that which is true, he refused to preach to or have communion with the unseparated people of Boston's Congregational church. In accord with Browne, who impugned those who worshipped in an Anglican parish, most English separatists refused communion with Anglicans, although they differed in the extent to which they were willing to pray with, partake in the Lord's supper with, and listen to sermons given by members of the Church of England. Barrowe stated that even to participate in an English service (since it was Roman) was to run counter to the Lord. Prior to being influenced by the thought of Jacob Arminius, Smyth believed it unlawful to hear an Anglican preacher. Williams condemned the Boston church for allowing its members to attend Anglican services while in the British Isles, and in Cotton's Letter Examined he criticized Cotton for saying that it is permissible to listen to a sermon in the Church of England but not to partake in the sacraments.[17] Like Barrowe, Canne, and Clarke, Roger Williams renounced communion with Anglicans. Barrowe contended that the Anglican ministry was unscriptural and illegitimate because it was based on political power. An authentic ministry cannot exist without a purified church. Furthermore, Barrowe condemned government salaries for the clergy, believing tax-supported compensation contrary to the pattern of free contributions initiated by Christ. On the basis of these principles Williams, like Clarke, condemned all established churches and state-supported ministries. In 1652 in The Hireling Ministry Williams appealed to the English Parliament not to salary ministers.[18]

Convinced that discipline was a more important mark of the church than the sacraments. Barrowe and Greenwood de-emphasized baptism and did not advocate re-baptism, even though Greenwood refused to have his son baptized by an Anglican priest. Furthermore, Greenwood declared that he was not an anabaptist.[19] Indeed, in 1607 when Smyth wrote Parallels, Censures, and Observation he condemned anabaptism as well as papism.[20] Two years later, however, Smyth was a full-fledged baptist, having immersed himself.[21] For him, believers' baptism replaced the signed covenant as the primary method of discipline and sign of membership. He no longer was convinced that a church is constituted on the basis of a covenant. Smyth viewed adult baptism as a logical consequence of separation and as the definitive indication of a free commitment, foreshadowing the next stage in the development of separatism and Williams's ultimate belief. Smyth's communication in Holland with the Waterland Mennonite Church is well documented; Williams's knowledge of and/or experience with the Continental anabaptists is not.

The state, as construed by Calvin, has both a moral and civil function. Government is to protect and support the true Christian religion, to defend both the doctrines and worship pattersn of the church, and to prevent (even suppress) heresy and idolatry. But it is not to domnate the church in a one-sided manner. Church officials are in charge of affairs of their institution. Even so, in The Institutes Calvin elevated the dignity of the magisterial position.[22] Whereas the separatists rejected Calvin's understanding of church polity and politics, Cartwright, Cotton, most presbyterians, and most congregationalists accepted it. In spite of other differences, Cartwright and Cotton advocated a Calvinistic doctrine of state and church in which the relationship is one of institutional distinctiveness but of close cooperation, even alignment. Thus, Cartwright and Cotton, unlike Williams, Clarke, and Canne, continued to argue for a national church and on behalf of an organic view of church and commnwealth. Like the Genevan reformer, as orthodox puritans they contended that church and state should be intimately related though distinct, and that the state exists, in part, to defend the church and therefore has the power to enforce the civil peace. Moreover, because Cartwright and Cotton believed (as Calvin did) that only God can differentiate between regenerate and reprobate, they accepted the mixed nature of the official church and resisted separation from the multitude.

Likewise, for most of Browne's adult life he maintained a Calvinistic understanding of the role of civil rulers in ecclesiastical affairs. Browne was an erastian, not a democratic, congregationalist.[23] In that sense, his precepts correlated (fifty years later) more closely with Cotton's views than with those of Williams who rejected politically-imposed religious conformity. Yet Browne was inconsistent in seeking a church of the most faithful while concurrently adhering to a religious uniformity imparted by a state church. On the one hand, he accepted the Genevan ideal of a church-state, adhered to the desire to reform the entire nation, and believed that the duty of the ruler is to enforce compliance with the true faith. The godly prince should procure reformation even it if means curtailing liberty. Browne acknowledged the inevitability of government interference in internal religious affairs, despite his insistence that there was no need for the church to await political approval to reform itself, indicating his interest was in reformation, not freedom, and in liberation of church form state, not vice versa. On the other hand, during his separatist phase he accepted limitations on magisterial dominion over the church. In spite of the fact that the prince has jurisdiction over secular concerns, his ecclesiastical authority is restricted. In the event of a conflict, the Lord rather than the prince must be obeyed. The monarch's authority is essentially civil; he lacks the right to intervene needlessly in religious affairs. The church need not depend on the power of the state. One explanation for the contradiction is that Browne's perspective, like that of Williams, differed over time.

Initially, Barrowe also accepted magisterial involvement in churchly affairs and the idea of a state church, irrespective of his call for a reformation without tarrying for any, including the monarch. In order to achieve reform, Barrowe admonished that the queen should advance true religion and suppress all heresy, idolatry, and false worship. Nevertheless, his views had been radicalized some time prior to his inquisition by the archbishop. By then, Barrowe specifically rejected the theory of the godly prince, believing scripture placed limits on the spiritual authority of the crown. He no longer asserted that a magistrate should maintain true religion by force. Smyth also changed his mind. Originally, Smyth asserted that the monarch was supreme over ecclesiastical in addition to civil matters when he wrote A Paterne of True Prayer in 1605, but within five years the self-baptist changed his views.[24]

The original separatists were among the first to deny to government the authority to punish heresy or idolatry. In a similar manner Williams sought to restrict the jurisdiction of both ecclesiastical and civil authorities. Williams was convinced that neither has a right to interfere in the realm of the other. The magistrate may enforce only the second table of the law, the minister the first. For Williams there is no such thing as a Christian merchant or prince. The ruler is the supreme civil authority, regardless of his religious convictions. The orthodoxy of his faith makes a civic leader no more, or no less, qualified for political office. And church leaders should avoid recourse to the power of government and law. Whereas other sectarians had opposed only the system in England, Williams condemned all state churches and all church-states as inherently antichristian.[25] For the body politic to interfere in religious affairs is to upset "the very foundations and roots of all true Christianity, and absolutely deny the Lord Jesus."[26] A church can be a true body of Christ only if it is without state support. For this reason, Williams took issue with the attempt to erect in Massachusetts a holy commonwealth, a position antagonistic to the professed goals of the leadership. As a separatist, Williams may have initially accepted th necessity for government-enforced discipline to keep the faithful in line; however, soon after arriving in Massachusetts in 1631, he rejected political interference in the realm of religion.

Calvin had taught both interdependence and independence between state and church, highlighting cooperation. By divine decree, man is "subject of two kinds of government"--one spiritual, the other civil; both are governed by God.[27] Even though each has a distinct function, Calvin was convinced that the two realms are intricately related. However, the distinction between the two is less clear than at first glance it appears. Calvin did not believe it possible for a church to be completely pure. Nor did Browne advocate unequivocal separation of religious from secular power or authority. While Browne was of the opinion that individual churches should defect from the state-controlled system, he never sought to dissociated ecclesiastical and political institutions, as Williams and Browne's successors in the seventeenth century understood it. Browne did not argue for religious liberty. Yet, paradoxically, Brownism was the breeding ground for the theory of absolute institutional separation, for the derivation for Williams's doctrine lies deep within the separatist heritage. In order to achieve toleration, Williams believed a complete divorce was necessary.

The second section of Williams's Bloudy Tenent accentuated the need for strict church-state separation, rebutting the Massachusetts defense of the Genevan pattern codified in the 1640s first in A Model of Church and Civil

Power and later in the Cambridge Platform. Williams alleged--counter to the non-separatists Calvin, Cartwright, and Cotton--that the Bible condemns an alliance of religion and politics and that coordination between such heavenly and earthly institutions is by its very nature antichristian. Williams distinguished between the two worlds more completely than did Calvin, Cartwright, Cotton, and the early English separatists. Williams interpreted literally the contention that there exist two distinct, unrelated spheres. For Williams the concern of the church is exclusively ecclesiastical, that of government solely civil.[28] It is improbable that such an absolute chasm has ever existed in human history, for separation can never be as complete as Williams sought since it would preclude interaction.

Browne wrote that "the Lordes kingdom is not by force."[29] He thought that ministers should disavow the power of the state to do their bidding. In general, all English separatists maintained that civil authority should be limited and government should not ascribe unduly patterns of worship for the citizenry. Yet prior to the 1640s religious toleration was only an incidental concern among separatists. Smyth was the only elder separatist who pleaded for freedom for non-separatists, and he did not advocate liberty when he wrote A Patern of True Prayer in 1605, even though he espoused that universal principle five years later in Propositions and Conclusions.[30] In the late 1630s, sometime after his banishment, Williams (like Clarke) adopted the overall baptist position, including the sectarian arguments for religious freedom. Thereafter, Williams gave priority to the issue of liberty over that of reformation. By the 1640s he held the view that each individual should have the unrestricted right to think for himself. The right to live as one wished, for Williams, was no longer limited to the elect but extended to all people. The first half of The Bloudy Tenent is a plea for soul liberty and an attack on the antichristian, bloody tenet of persecution which seeks to suppress "errant" consciences by force. Aware that the truth was yet to be known, by the 1640s Williams believed that in the state (but not in the church) error should be tolerated, even though a decade before he sought a completely pure church that would exclude people unable to achieve his standard of perfection. No ecclesiastical or governmental official is qualified to determine the veracity of another's faith.

Browne advocated Christocracy, not democracy. He taught an indwelling Christ working through all believers equally. The irony is that even though Browne envisioned an absolute monarchy, in the long run his ideas about separation encouraged the trend toward ecclesiastical self-government and eventually individual freedom. Browne's doctrine of the church was based on the supposition that the Christian ideal is a monarchy in which Jesus reigns over His flock. As Perry Miller observed, Browne "recognized the danger in the centrifugal democracy of his polity and frankly trusted in the civil power to keep it in check."[31] In response to the fear and concern that "factions & heresies might grow," Browne said, "I answere that the ciuil Magistrate must restraine that licentiousness." Williams, on the other hand, preferred no specific form of government. He would have accepted any secular polity that allowed religious liberty whether a monarchy, an oligarchy, or a constitutional democracy.[32] Williams professed that his call for liberty was not absolute and should not be misconstrued to justify indiscriminate license and that people have no right to revolt against unjust rule. In civil concerns a Christian is obligated to obey the powers that be, even if they be pagan or popish. But that obedience is limited to social behavior; it does not include matters of conscience. On these points Williams differed little from his precursors.

Yet Williams did more than merely expound on the thoughts of those who inhabited the religious underground of the preceding century. Although based on separatist ecclesiology and theology, his world view was a radicalization--but not necessarily a democratization--of sixteenth century dissident thought. For instance, the mature Williams of the 1640s and '50s differed from his predecessors--even from the youthful Williams--in advocating civil tolerance for the unregenerate. Secondly, while the original separatists were concerned chiefly with church polity, Williams's primary interest was religious liberty and its implications for government and society. And whereas the early separatists condemned only one particular church, Williams sought to keep distinct all ecclesiastical and civil entities. He helped lay the groundwork for new approaches in politics as in religion. Intellectually Williams carried the principles of religious separatism from the theological to the social level by applying the ideas of his precursors to the courtroom as well as the pew. One reason he was able to do so is that his theologically-based arguments were more readily adaptable to political concerns than were the narrow ecclesiastical doctrines of his dissident predecessors.

The early separatists sought to make a place for their circumscribed congregations in a society intolerant of religious diversity. Their concern was purity for themselves and their colleagues. Even so, because they were confronted with substantial resistance from an overwhelming, firmly-imbedded erastian order, Williams's precursors were unable to direct their energy creatively toward development of a new national order. They focused on protecting themselves and their underground communities. As persecuted and notorious sects, they were forced to be concerned with toleration for themselves but had not reached a theoretical understanding of the enlarged and more far-reaching concept of widespread or universal liberty. Unaware of the many implications of their ideas, the first separatists were unable to move, as Williams subsequently did, from a congregational-centered to a national outlook. In Europe they defined their position in opposition to a long established, hierarchical order. Prior to the English Civil Wars, they were unable legally and freely to practice their faith in England.

Nevertheless, in America Williams and later separatists were able to break away from the past and from the old cuius regio thinking.[33] The width of the Atlantic Ocean was so great that the remnants of sacerdotalism could not easily cross it. Massachusetts notwithstanding, there was more freedom in America to believe and live as one pleased than in the tightly-regulated church-state structure that existed prior to the execution of Charles I. There were fewer inhibitions, so less reason to disguise intentions. A newly discovered continent provided immigrants with an opportunity to realize ideals which had been suppressed in Europe. In New England Williams and the baptists were able for the first time to carry out a comprehensive and positive plan for ideal Christian communities, thereby playing a significant role in the shaping of modern society. Without the king and the Anglican church they were able to act boldly and freely upon deep-rooted convictions. In the words of Elizabeth Radmacher, "the free atmosphere of the American scene provided a choice opportunity for the propagation of the free church principles." But Radmacher overstates the case when she writes that "while there was no development of new doctrine, there was a place to practice that which had previously been restricted by established church systems."[34] The tolerationist works of Williams and of Clarke made a significant impact in England as well as in New England. Yet Radmacher is correct in the stress she places on the opportunity that America provided for dissident separatist attitudes to flourish.

In 1646 even the Presbyterian Thomas Edwards acknowledged grudgingly that "all Errors take Sanctuary in Independency, flie there [i.e., to New England] and are safe, as the Chickens under the wing of the Hen." And in a statement often quoted to substantiate the charge that Massachusetts did not allow freedom of conscience, Williams implicitly recognizes the difference between old and New England: "Surely, if the same New English churches were in Old England, they could not meet without persecution, which therefore in old England they avoid by frequenting the way of church worship which in New England they persecute, the parishes."[35] In part this was because separation was the sine qua non of American reality. Geography detached the colonies from the motherland. Circumstances necessarily limited the immediate impact of English leaders, institutions, and ideas. The transatlantic influence of the Church of England was confined from the beginning. The distance from home played into the hands of America's first prominent radicals. As a result, various aspects of puritan and separatist doctrine (e.g., voluntarism, gathered churches, covenants, lay participation in the governance of the church, election of officers, dissociation from the Anglican Church, and the principle of separation of church and state) gained wider, deeper acceptance in New England than in the mother country. So Loren Beth has said that "separation is an American achievement."[36]

In estimating Williams influence, W. K. Jordan concluded that "Williams's most significant contribution to the theory of toleration is to be found in his masterly argument against the interference of the State in religious life."[37] Jordan's observation is based on the assumption that Williams's insistence on liberty followed from his thesis of separation. After his rustication Williams seems to have moved form a preoccupation with purity of faith and ecclesiastical discipline to concern for civil tolerance and understanding. On the one hand, Williams agreed with Cotton that only a few elect would be saved, declaring that only by separating church and state would the saints be free to escape the lamentable doom of humanity. On the other hand, Williams condemned persecution by government of anyone for religious reasons. His understanding of the nature of conscience and of church-state relations in that sense differed from that of the Massachusetts establishment. Williams was a Calvinist, but he advocated a revolutionary view: complete separation of church and state. Williams position was even more extreme than that of most separatists on that issue. He rejected the ambiguity of the Reformed position regarding church-state relations while simultaneously remaining a Calvinist theologically, except in the realm of ecclesiology.

Roger Williams argued for disestablishment and embraced freedom of thought. He was willing to tolerate all types of religious ideas and thus to respect his neighbor's right to his own beliefs. Through both his writings and the policies of Rhode Island, Williams became a leading spokesman for government-enforced liberty of conscience for all, advocating civil (but not soteriological) "permission of the most Paganish, Jewish, Turkish, or Antichristian consciences and worships"--a position anathema to most of his contemporaries as well as to previous generations of separatists.[38] For instance, neither Cromwell nor Milton ever advocated complete liberty for all. Yet Williams was willing to tolerate even some of the most blasphemous, heretical, peculiar, and dangerous views. Among dissident separatists, as well as others, Williams was unusual in including Jewish people. He believed that by extending toleration to Jewish people two objectives could be accomplished: England's persecution of the Jews would be atoned and propagation of the Gospel would be hastened. However, he may have extended civil liberty to them primarily because he thought that freedom was the most effective way to evangelize among them.

Theologically orthodox, Williams did not reject the predestinarian distinction between elect and reprobate. He viewed the masses of people as outcasts and considered most of them among the reprobate. Yet, paradoxically, because of such pessimism, Williams was willing to allow all the world's inhabitants the prerogatives of state citizenship, in part because most of them were predestined to hell anyway. On account of his Calvinistic faith, rather than in spite of it, Williams believed that the unregenerate should not be controlled by law, but deserve instead unrestrained latitude. Williams was willing to endure even the views he did not accept, because as a good Calvinist he knew he was right and they were wrong. Moreover, he believed that the true Christian church must be radically different from any government or nation; religion is a higher way to go.

It is important to note that analysis of Roger Williams's views is made more complex because his doctrines changed over time. The Bloudy Tenent represents Williams's mature views regarding liberty and toleration, and thus differed in matter of degree from his pre-banishment ideas. During the 1630s Williams was literalistic and absolute, but by 1644 (the year he composed The Bloudy Tenent) his demeanor mellowed and he become more tolerant of others' opinions, though he was no less certain of his own correctness. Consequently, less than a decade after his deportation from Massachusetts, Williams asserted publicly a willingness to defend the civil rights of those with whom which he disagreed--an uncommon step even in the era of the Protectorate. Thus, he assisted in the consummation of the three-tier movement from conformity to toleration to liberty.

Chapter 7

Endnotes

[1]Williams, Hireling Ministry, ed. Miller, Complete Writings, VII, 219.

[2]Ibid., 183.

[3]John Calvin, Institutes of the Christian Religion, ed. John T. McNeill (Philadelphia, 1977; Geneva, 1559), trans. Ford L. Battles, II, 1485. See William A. Mueller, Church and State in Luther and Calvin: A Comparative Study (Nashville, 1954), 138.

[4]Smyth, A Paterne of True Prayer, ed. Whitley, Works of John Smyth, I, 166.

[5]Smyth, Propositions and Conclusions, ed. Whitley, Works of John Smyth, II, 734-37.

[6]Williams dealt with the issue of qualifications for church membership in Cottons Letter Examined, ed. Guild, Complete Writings, I, 86.

[7]Calvin, Institutes, II, 1021-22. See Paul D. L. Avis, The Church in the Theology of the Reformers (Atlanta, 1981), 61-62.

[8]Williams, Cottons Letter Examined, ed. Guild, Complete Writings, I, 5.

[9]Smyth, Principles and Inferences, ed. Whitley, Works of John Smyth, I, 252.

[10]Barrowe, Trve Description, ed. Carlson, Writings, 1587-90, III, 222.

[11]Ibid., II, 15, 24, and 463. There were some differences among the separatists as to attitude toward Anglicans. Robinson seems to have been somewhat more tolerant concerning contact, but even the Pilgrim pastor shunned those who he felt were corrupt.

[12]Smyth, Paralleles, Censvres, ed. Whitley, Works, II, 337.

[13]Robinson, A Justification of Separation, ed. Ashton, Works, II, 16.

[14]On this specific point they disagreed, even though in general Smyth's tenets were a stepping-stone to Williams's.

[15]Barrowe, Briefe Discoverie, ed. Carlson, Writings, 1587-90, III, 302.

[16]Smyth, Parallels, Censures, ed. Whitley, Works of John Smyth, I, 515-16.

[17]Williams, Cottons Letter Examined, ed. Guild, Complete Writings, I, 110.

[18]Williams, Hireling Ministry, ed. Miller, Complete Writings, VII, 88.

[19]Greenwood, "Greenwood's Examination," ed. Carlson, Writings of Greenwood, IV, 26.

[20]Smyth, Parallels, Censures, ed. Whitley, Works of John Smyth, I, 135.

[21]See Robinson, A Just and Necessarie Apologie, ed. Ashton, Works of Robinson, II, 48 for a description of Smyth's baptism of himself.

[22]Calvin, Institutes, II, 1489-90.

[23]See Frederick Powicke, Robert Browne, 79.

[24]Smyth, Propositions and Conclusions, ed. Whitley, Works of John Smyth, II, 746.

[25]By the 1640s Williams attached only limited merit to formal worship and church institutions of any kind. Philosophically and practically Williams was opposed to establishment of an official national church--be it congregational, presbyterian, or episcopal. For him, the very concept is problematic.

[26]Williams, The Blovdy Tenent, ed. Caldwell, Complete Writings, III, 367-68.

[27]Calvin, Institutes, IV, xx.1.

[28]For Williams, the state is essentially without religious power; the church need not be concerned with civil affairs.

[29]Browne, Reformation without Tarying, ed. Peel and Carlson, Writings, I, 161-62.

[30]Smyth, Propositions and Conclusions, ed. Whitley, Works of John Smyth, II, 735.

[31]Miller, Orthodoxy in Massachusetts, 64.

[32]Williams's praise for the Cromwellian Protectorate is an exception to his general view regarding governmental structure.

[33]Cuius regio, eius religio may be translated as "whose is the government, his is the religion," meaning that citizens are required to adopt the faith of their ruler.

[34]Radmacher, 85.

[35]Edwards, Gangraena, 62; and Williams, Cottons Letter Examined, ed. Guild, Complete Writings, I, 111.

[36]Loren P. Beth, The American Theory of Church and State (Gainesville, Florida, 1958), 33-34.

[37]Jordan, III, 476.

[38]Williams, Bloudy Tenent, ed. Caldwell, Complete Writings, III.

CONCLUSION

Having begun in the 1580s as an idea in the minds of a handful of disenchanted ministers, within four decades separatism had expanded to include an entire network of true believers in England, Holland, and America. By Williams's day, separatism had become a movement with which the leaders in both the old and the new worlds were forced to reckon. During the mid-sixteenth century a deep-seated fear developed among the early separatists over government encroachment into religious affairs that led in the following century to the emergence of complete separation of church and state as a prominent issue. Williams, a self-proclaimed troubler of conscience, was a significant figure in the culmination of that far-reaching demand for differentiation. His separatist religious views evolved in such a way as to make a vital contribution to the history of the development of America's must fundamental principle, church-state separation, and of its corollary: religious conscience.

In brief, my purpose has been to demonstrate that the separatists and their better-known offspring, the baptists, played an important role in the formation and development of New England's social order; that the doctrines of the first separatists were a major source for Williams's beliefs; that Williams's views were an unusual or radical application of the principles of those earlier separatist; that separatist thought underwent a change from a narrowly conceived religious concept to a much broader social principle as it moved across the Atlantic Ocean; that Williams and his precursors helped alter the relationship between church and state in old and New England; and finally that Williams's understanding of religious liberty was based on a doctrine of separation that evolved from his separatist world view.

First, it is important to note that Americans are indebted to the thinkers mentioned herein. The rights and liberties enjoyed in the United States today are, in part, a result of the creativity and courage exhibited by the separatists and other dissenters. That an American citizen is relatively free to attend the worship service of his choice, to reject ecclesiastical dictates, to criticize leaders, and to organize an unorthodox church or sect can be credited, in large measure, to their inspiration and work. The contribution of Roger Williams and of the separatists to the genesis of early American culture should not be undervalued.[1]

Though unpopular and insignificant at its inception, the separatist movement was fraught with long-range implications. From the teachings of Williams and his predecessors new perspectives emerged. The separatists and baptists were instrumental in engendering such farsighted principles as election of church officers, ecclesiastical government by consent of the people, a democratic or congregational polity, denominationalism, separation of church and state, freedom of conscience, and limitations on magisterial and clerical authority. In particular, the ultimate outcome, church-state dissociation, deviated substantially from the norms that dominated the age, placing the baptists and others at the forefront of the free church movement that ensued as a logical consequence of the initial movement merely to purify the Church of England. The contribution of the separatists was vital in the development of the Anglo-American way of life and culture, in spite of their small numbers and limited personal influence. Unfortunately, few people today are aware of the significance of Williams and the separatists. The Protestant Reformation, the Enlightenment, and various other intellectual and religious trends (as well as socio-economic factors) are generally acknowledged to have been influential in the germination of contemporary understandings of religion and politics. Many subsequent modern-day developments contributed to such widely-accepted notions as church-state separation, religious liberty, denominationalism, congregational church polity, and political democracy. Yet, separatism (which came first chronologically) necessarily served as a stepping-stone for much Enlightenment thought. Nearly forty years before John Locke published in 1690 his plea for toleration and promulgated certain self-evident rights and liberties, Williams had demanded tolerance and liberty for all religious dissenters. The history of separatism demonstrates the truth of the axiom that religiously-motivated enthusiasts often are the first to pioneer new paths and traditions and to break through the barriers of convention and misunderstanding.

The England into which Williams was born was ecclesiastically a relatively unified, undenominationalized society. There was little room for diversity; dissent was curtailed. In England, the established church monopolized religious observance; free churches were non-existent; only a single Protestant church was allowed to operate. Freedom to join the church of one's choice was not a viable option. Membership in the official church and attendance at its worship services was compulsory. Groups which held unauthorized private observances did so clandestinely.[2] In comparison, modern America is a multi-denominational, pluralistic society, consisting of a myriad of denominations and sects, in which in theory at least all churches coexist as equals before the law and operate solely on a voluntary basis. Unlike the first separatists, we are free to leave one church and join another (even an unpopular religious group) without suffering civil penalties. Today, a multitude of independent sects and denominations have become an integral aspect of the Christian way, but that is only a recent reality. As Sidney Mead has pointed out, denominationalism is a "peculiarly American" phenomenon.[3]

The second concern has been the extent to which the sources for Williams's precepts, especially his ecclesiology and political theory, lie within the separatist religious tradition. Although no one would argue that Williams obtained his beliefs ex nihilo, few scholars have even noted the depths of his theological commitment to separatism and of his theological disagreement with Massachusetts. Williams was influenced by the early separatists and other puritans. He was able to employ fruitfully the ideas of his predecessors in order to lay the groundwork for unconventional approaches to God and government. Williams was primarily a controversialist, able to synthesize ideas borrowed from others into a compelling series of emotional arguments designed to gain attention for his cause. His insight into the most profound of issues coupled with his dogged and brash determination to pursue ideas to their logical conclusions made Williams a moving force in the spiritual epic of America.

A third point regards the difficult question of whether Williams was instrumental in the institution and advancement of a new, distinctly more radical doctrine of separation. I have uncovered considerable evidence to support the position that Williams worked with the earlier religious notions in such a way as to create and espouse a more extreme, more pervasive, and eventually more tolerant understanding of separateness. From his predecessors Williams inherited certain beliefs about church and state. He then proceeded to move separatism from a forward to an unmitigated position based on those prior ideas. Whereas the early nonconformists were less than full separatists, Williams evolved into an ardent baptist who argued stubbornly for unconditional separation of church and state. Williams was, in fact, convinced that he had carried the policy of reformation without tarrying to its logical limits and conclusions in his advocacy of dissociation of church and state, believers' baptism, and rejection of prayer with"unregenerate people," including wives and children who had not been saved. Indeed, in Providence he ended up withdrawing from a baptist church he himself had founded.[4]

From a comparison of the works of Williams and the early separatists clear distinctions emerge. Williams's precursors were a harried minority who found themselves in a defensive position vis-a-vis the English establishment. Circumstances had pushed them, willy-nilly, to separate. Unable in the 1570s to convert the English monarch to the Genevan ideal, the Brownists and Barrowists were forward puritans who felt compelled to break with the official church. But they were ecclesiastical, not political, innovators. The political and social milieu was such that the first separatists were unable to practice their faith openly even though they were intellectually creative. They discovered a novel form of church organization (congregationalism), but did not foresee the need for alternative definitions of government's role in English society. They viewed separation from the national church merely as a temporary, short-run, spiritual undertaking.

In contrast, from his haven in Rhode Island, Williams was much more provocative and bold. He took the offensive against all church-state establishments by promulgating a new vision and a comprehensive counterproposal to the status quo. His was a comprehensive, fresh understanding of the nature, purpose, and relationship between church and commonwealth. Williams laid the ideological foundation for emergence of the concept of an impartial, secular state which allows a multitude of denominations and sects to flourish unmolested. He did so by moving separatism intellectually from a preoccupation with personal, congregational, and purely spiritual freedom to embracement of broad-based moral/political principles. The state is, Williams believed, a secular institution of divine origin that lacks any spiritual role or significance since it is based on a non-religious covenant. Governments should operate independent of the beliefs of the citizenry and the ecclesiastical dictates of religious leaders. The function of the magistrate should be civil, never spiritual.

Preoccupied with the crisis of the moment and lacking clear historical models, Williams's predecessors were unable to conceptualize the broad philosophical and social implications of their newly emerging ideas and actions. Even in their maturity the early nonconformists did not realize the full import of their theological views. They failed to envision a comprehensive organizational plan. In spite of attempts to dissociated from the established church, none of the original separatists arrived at Williams's unyielding principle of complete separation. Under the overwhelming pressures of the moment, they sought only to obtain freedom to worship God for themselves by disengaging from one particular, state-controlled church.[5] By carrying the separatist position to its limits, Williams imparted to the new world something special, unique, and social as well as religious.

Separatism did not spring forth in the colonies de novo. Most puritan and separatist concepts (e.g., gathered churches, church covenants, congregational autonomy and polity, and limitation of membership to the regenerate) originated in England and matured in America. The ideas of puritan radicalism travelled with various separatists and baptists, most notably Williams, across the ocean. In that sense, separatism, in New England, especially as carried forth by the baptists, was an extrapolation on the Brownism of sixteenth century England; it was, therefore, a foreign-bred rather than an indigenous case. Yet with Williams's conversion in the 1630s from puritanism to rigid separatism, Anglo-American nonconformity entered a new era. The moment he disembarked at Boston radical strains of thought burst forth.

Another question concerns the transformation of separatist thought as it crossed the Atlantic Ocean. In a new land where settlers were carving out new lives based on new visions, separatism reached its culmination and its concerns permeated the culture. Having undergone a period of incubation in

Europe, separatism began to bloom in New England soon after arrival. In the unfamiliar surroundings of America, the separatist spirit soon became a potent, lively, and attractive social force, gaining acceptance over time and growing beyond its narrow sectarian soil.

Insofar as emigration was a natural form of separation, the trek across the ocean provided the sectarians with a solution to their dilemma of being unable to worship as they pleased without incrimination. The Atlantic was wide enough to stay the encroachment of sacerdotalism, thereby facilitating the break with the English establishment. There was more freedom in the new land for the practice of unconventional theological doctrines than in tightly-controlled England. In the American colonies radical puritans like Williams had an opportunity to implement and conceptualize a comprehensive and positive plan for society. Despite resistance during the early years in Massachusetts, in New England they had a role to play in the shaping of entire communities; for the first time being able to implement many of their theologically-based ideas. People in North America were receptive, in that they were less concerned with hierarchies and established ways. The crown and episcopacy were too far removed to control the situation.

Since Williams and the baptists met with less resistance in America, they possessed an unusual opportunity to work positively toward the formation of forward-looking communities. The negative element of government encroachment was minimal and America provided space to move away from limitations. In such a relatively uninhibited environment, energy could be used in creative development rather than in mere resistance to the status quo. There was opportunity in America for the rise of an untried democratic political and religious order. In Rhode Island (and eventually in Massachusetts) Williams, Clarke, and their associates carried to completion doctrines which had originated across the ocean in the land of their birth as essentially religious concerns.

In a new society with a developing, uncalcified church-state structure, Williams was able to focus his energy imaginatively in the construction and advancement of lasting social principles. Rather than merely responding negatively to the standing order, he averred something positive--complete separation. It is true that the colony of Massachusetts was unresponsive to his demands; however, in Rhode Island Williams was able to achieve his heart's desire. There in that haven for separatists Williams was able to apply ideas concerning complete freedom of conscience to a concrete community.

The relationship between religion and politics underwent many changes during this period. From the time of Constantine in the fourth century until the adoption of the United States Constitution in the eighteenth century--a period of more than fourteen hundred years--the medieval idea of society as a corpus christianum prevailed. Tensions notwithstanding, in Europe during the Middle Ages unity between church and state was based on Christian catholicity centered on Rome. Even the Protestant Reformation did not fundamentally change that prevailing cultural predisposition toward national uniformity throughout Europe; from the sixteenth through the eighteenth centuries the policy of cuius regio, eius religio reigned. That a government could allow religious divergences to coexist within its territory without courting disaster was, for most people, inconceivable. An alliance of church and state was the heritage of early modern Europe. Political and religious liberty were severely limited. The activities and writings of the English separatists helped shift that centuries-old alliance into a relationship of separation.

It was in America in the late eighteenth century, that a novel constitutional principle--separation of church and state--gained wide acceptance and became the law of the land.[6] Remarkably, a century-and-a half before religious liberty became widely accepted and made a constitutional right, the farseeing Williams had advocated complete separation and freedom of conscience, an ideal that has never been fully realized. As a movement religious separatism quickly died, but its basic principles survived through such doctrines as separation of church and state and on account of the ardor of successive generations of Baptists, Quakers, and Congregationalists. Furthermore, one effect of separatism--on the American milieu--was to enhance the strength of the separatist impulse by making the basic principle of separation axiomatic despite its eventual dissolution as an issue or movement.[7] In colonial America, the sectarians battled for a revolutionary new concept: separation from all established churches rather than only from the Roman, Anglican, Presbyterian or Congregational versions of the true Christian faith and polity as the separatists sought to do. Within a few decades the distance across the ocean mitigated distinctions between most forms of separating and non-separating congregationalism.

Long before Williams graduated from college, other separatists had developed a somewhat new doctrine of the church. Accordingly, Williams's contribution toward the intellectual development of the concept of separation was primarily in the realm of politics and church-state relations. His ideas had profound political implications, even though his work is deeply religious and his training was as a pastor and theologian. While he did not elaborate a detailed political theory, Williams sounded the trumpet for abolition of an old system of church-state relations and formation of new interactions. In contradistinction to the original separatists, who abandoned the desire to reform the entire nation, Williams issued for America a death warrant for erastianism and of any kind proclaimed a series of principles that became the foundation for a new world order. He laid the groundwork for uncommon approaches in politics as in religion. He transmitted an important set of fixed principles to a world experiencing budding democracy. Readily adaptable to American society, his tolerationist views became classic expressions of the American ethos. Grounded in the foundations which Williams laid, his spiritual descendents on both sides of the Atlantic were able to build churches and communities based on new-fashioned ecclesiastical and social concepts.

The separatists played a significant spiritual and intellectual role in the development of a comprehensive tolerationist perspective even though they were instrumental in only one aspect of an entire movement in the seventeenth century towards religious liberty. During the eighteenth century, Deists, Quakers, Baptists, and other religious groups intensified the assault on civil and ecclesiastical authority which the religious separatists had begun two centuries before.

Finally, the principles of civil liberty and tolerance evolved significantly during this time. The baptist theory of toleration of unusual religious ideas and sects sprang from the belief that the church must be free from state control. Although in the beginning separation was not intended to bring about either liberty or toleration, eventually it contributed greatly to the growth of those principles. Both were consequences of the decision to separate, insofar as "coming out" meant that loyalty to God and adherence to conscience takes precedence over obedience to worldly authority. The attack on government intervention in spiritual affairs led naturally to advocacy of liberty of conscience for all. By the 1640s and '50s many baptists were fervent tolerationists, as Williams's uncompromising views demonstrate. By the early 1640s Williams believed that religious freedom was based on the precept of separation--a doctrine that grew naturally from his separatist heritage. In the Bloudy Tenent, Williams declared that conscience is beyond the jurisdiction of either church or state. By then, if not before, he was convinced that soul liberty was possible only if the cross and the sword remain completely distinct. Williams's assumption, shared by other baptists, was that the realm of faith is outside the jurisdiction of institutional government.

Regarding Williams, there is considerable disagreement as to his historical importance. Whether Williams was the first on either side of the Atlantic to demand in writing the right of private judgment for people of all religious persuasions is contestable. The history of the evolution of the doctrines of liberty and toleration is complex. Obviously there was no one author or spokesman for either cause. The change to leniency was rooted in England in the separatist reaction of the 1580s and the radical baptist response of the 1640s and in America in the freedom which ensued form geographical separation of the colonies from the motherland. Nonetheless, Williams gave to liberty a doctrine of complete institutional separation, making freedom not just acceptable but a theological necessity. To study Williams is to gain powerful insight into the American past. No other seventeenth century write reveals so much about the development of American attitudes toward church, state, freedom, and civil rights. Through his life and tracts, Williams left an indelible impression on a new land. Many of his "dangerous opinions" have become classic expressions of contemporary Anglo-American culture. Most importantly, Williams provided meaningful theological reasons for what eventually became a significant aspect of the

American way--free churches in a free society. Williams made a telling contribution to a world experiencing the birth pangs of voluntarism, liberty, and democracy. The structure of his thought was readily adaptable to the newly-emerging American culture. On the intellectual foundations which he laid, as an innovator and as a troubler of conscience, future generations of Americans were able to build a society based on a novel, religiously-inspired understanding of church-state relations.

Conculsion

Endnotes

[1]Modern society has inherited much from the separatists, irrespective of their small numbers and limited influence in their day. Their insight and bravery made it possible for future generations to experience more freedom. However, the degree to which liberty exists or has existed in the United States is disputable. Complete, uninhibited religious freedom has never existed in America, or anywhere else, despite the assurances of the U.S. Constitution. Often new religious movements and leaders have been persecuted and misunderstood.

[2]While a national church has never existed in America, in some states within the U.S. tax-supported churches persisted until the beginning of the nineteenth-century. Official established churches lingered in Connecticut until 1818 and in Massachusetts through 1833.

[3]Sidney E. Mead, The Lively Experiment: The Shaping of Christianity in America (New York, 1963), 36.

[4]Whether Williams was the first Englishman to argue unequivocally, on religious grounds, for complete separation is disputable. Nevertheless, while the activities and beliefs of the Elizabethan separatists were innovative and set a precedent for engendering new approaches, Williams's principle of total separation was a revolutionary departure both theologically and socially from the views of his predecessors. Williams presented separatism in its most extreme form, demanding dissociation from all established churches and from all attempts at government encroachment. He was, for this reason, a leader of a new, more advanced wave of puritan dissent as well as a willing conduit for the essentialities of the orthodox Christian faith.

[5]Williams's view should be distinguished from that of his predecessors on this point. Only Smyth approached Williams's notion of liberty for all believers to practice their faith apart from magisterial interference. Unlike Williams, most separatists were unaware of the corollary doctrine of government autonomy stressing freedom from ecclesiastical controls. The forerunners rebelled against the English religious system, hence against certain ethical and ecclesiastical aspects of orthodox Calvinism, but the ultimate meaning was made obvious only by Williams's willingness to pursue separatist notions relentlessly to unorthodox conclusions.

[6]This is not to say that the distinction between church and state is solely a modern phenomena, but it is to assert that the doctrine of separation of church and commonwealth was pioneered in America and that it was foreshadowed in the life and thought of Williams.

[7]Withdrawal from the Anglican Church having been achieved with the journey across the Atlantic, in New England, separatism was an issue irrelevant to the post-Williams generation. Yet the legacy of separation of church and state became indispensable.

BIBLIOGRAPHY

Adamson, J. H. and H. F. Folland. Sir Harry Vane: His Life and Times (1613-1662) Boston, 1973.

Ainsworth, Henry. A Defence of the Holy Scriptures, Worship and Ministerie. [Amsterdam], 1609.

Ainsworth, Henry. The Communion of Saincts. Amsterdam, 1642.

Ainsworth, Henry. Counterpoyson, Considerations touching the points. [Amsterdam], 1608.

[Ainsworth, Henry and Francis Johnson]. An Apologie or Defence of Such True Christians as are Commonly (but Unjustly) Called Brownists: Against Such Imputations as Are Layed upon Them by the Heads and Doctors of the University of Oxford. . . [Amsterdam], 1604.

Alexander, H.G. Religion in England 1558-1662 London, 1968.

Ames, William. A Manvdvction for Mr. Robinson, and such as consent with him in private communion, to lead them on to public. Dort, 1614.

Ames, William. The Marrow of Theology, Drawn out of the Holy Scriptures, and the Interpreters thereof, and brought into Method. Amsterdam, 1628.

Ames, William. A Second Manvdvction for Mr. Robinson. Or a conformation of the former, in an answer to his manumission. Dort, 1615.

Anonymous. An Apologie of the Churches in New-England. Boston, 1643.

Anonymous. Zeal Examined: Or, A Discourse for Liberty of Conscience in Matters of Religion. London, 1652.

Ashley, Maurice. England in the Seventeenth Century Baltimore, 1952.

Ashley, Maurice. Oliver Cromwell and His World NY, 1972.

Ashton, Robert. The English Civil War: Conservatism and Revolution, 1603-1649 NY, 1979.

Aylmer, G. E., ed., The Interregnum: The Quest for Settlement 1646-1660 London, 1972.

Aylmer, G. E., ed., The Levellers in the English Revolution Ithaca, 1975.

Baillie, Robert. Anabaptisme the True Fountaine of Independency, Brownisme, Antinomy, Familisme, and most of the other errors which for The Time doe Trouble the Church of England unsealed. London, 1647.

Baillie, Robert. A Dissuasive from the Errours of the Time. London, 1645.

Baillie, Robert. The Letters and Journals of Robert Baillie A.M.: Principal of the University of Glasgow. 3 vols. ed. David Laing. Edinburgh, 1841-42.

Ball, John. An Answer to Two Treatises of Mr. I. Can . . . The former called, A Necessitie of Separation from the Church of and . . . The other, A Stay against Straying. London, 1642.

Barbour, Hugh. The Quakers in Puritan England New Haven, 1964.

Barbour, James and Thomas Quirk, eds., Essays on Puritans and Puritanism by Leon Howard Albuquerque, NM, 1986.

Barker, Arthur. Milton and the Puritan Dilemma 1641-1660 Toronto, 1942.

Barrowe, Henry. A Brief Discoverie of the False Church. [Dort], 1590.

Barrowe, Henry. A Refutation of Mr. Giffard's Reasons Concerning our Purposes in the Practise of the Truth of the Gospel of Christ. Dort, 1591.

Barrowe, Henry. A Trve Description out of the Worde of God, of the Visible Church. [Dort], 1589.

[Barrowe Henry et. al.] Mr. Henry Barrowes Platform. Which may serve, as a Preparative to purge away Prelatisme: with some other parts of Poperie. . . [London], 1611.

Barrowe, Henry. The First Part of the Platforme, Penned by that worthy servant of Jesus Christ, and Blessed witnes of his most Holy Ordinances, to the Losse of Life: Mr. Henry Barrowe. Dort, 1590.

Barrowe, Henry and John Greenwood. A Collection of Certain Letters and Conferences Lately Passed betwixt Certaine Preachers and Two Prisoners in the Fleet. [Dort], 1590.

Barrowe, Henry and John Greenwood. A Collection of Certaine Sclaunderous Articles Gyven out by the Bisshops against Such Faithfull Christians as They Now Unjustly Deteye in Their Prisons, Togeather with the Answere of the Saide Prisoners Therunto. . . [Dort], 1590.

Barrowe, Henry and John Greenwood. A Plaine Refutation of M. Giffords Books,Intituled, A Short Treatise gainst the Donatistes of England. [Dort], 1590.

Barrowe, Henry and John Greenwood. The Examinations of Henry Barrowe, John Greenwood and John Penrie before the High Commissioners and Lordes of the Counsel. Penned by the Prisoners Themselves before Their Deathes. [Dort], c.1593-95.

Bellamy, John. The Tudor Law of Treason: An Introduction London, 1979.

Bernard, Richard. Certain Positions held and maintained by some Godly ministers of the Gospel against those of the Separation; and namely against Barrowe and Greenwood.

Bernard, Richard. Christian Advertisements and Counsels of Pease. Also Dissuasions from the Separatist's Schism, commonly called Brownisme. London, 1608.

Bernard, Richard. Plaine Euidences: the Chvrch of England is Apostolicall; the Separation Schismatical. Directed against Mr. Ainsworth, the Separatist, and Mr. Smyth, the Se-baptist. London, 1610.

Bradford, William. A dialogue or the sume of a Conference between some younge men borne in New England and Sundery Ancient men that came out of holland and hold England Ann dom 1648," Publications of the Colonial Society of Massachusetts. Boston, 1920.

Bradford, William. History of Plymouth Plantation, 1620-1647. ed. Worthingon C. Ford. Boston, 1912.

Bredwell, Stephen. The Rasing of the Fovndations of Brovvnisme Wherein, Against All the Writings of the Principall Maters of that sect, those chiefe conclusions in the next page, are, . . .purposely handled, and soundly preoued. London, 1588.

Brown, Louise F. The Political Activities of the Baptists and Fifth Monarchy Men in England During the Interregnum London, 1911.

Browne, Robert. An ansvvere to Master Cartvvright His Letter For Ioyning with the English Churches whereunto the true copie of his sayde letter is annexed. London, 1585.

Browne, Robert. A Booke which Sheweth the Life and Manners of all Trve Christians, and howe vnlike they are vnto Turkes and Papistes, and Heathen folke. Middelburg, 1592.

Browne, Robert. A "New Years Guift": An Hitherto Lost Treatise by Robert Browne, The Father of Congregationalism. In the form of a Letter to his uncle Mr. Flowers (December 31, 1588), ed. Champlin Burrage. London, 1904.

Browne, Robert. A Treatise of Reformation without Tarying fo Anie, and of the Wickednesse of those Preachers which will not reforme till the Magistrate commaunde or compell them. Middelburg, 1582.

Browne, Robert. A True and Short Declaration, Both of the Gathering and Joyning Together of Certaine Persons, and also of the Lamentable Breach and Division which fell amongst them. Middelburg, 1583.

Burton, Henry. A Vindication of Churches Commonly called Independent. London, 1644.

Calvin, John. Institutes of the Christian Religion. trans. Ford L. Battles. Geneva, 1559 edition. Philadelphia, 1960.

Canne, John, et. al. A Narrative Wherein is faithfully set forth the Sufferings of John Canne, Wentworth Day, John Clarke . . .called, as their New Book saith, Fifth Monarchy Men, that is how eight of them were taken . . .as they were in the worship of God . . .and sent prisoners to the Counter. London, 1658.

Canne, John. A Necessitie of Separation from the Church of England, proved by the Nonconformists Principles. Amsterdam, 1634.

Canne, John. A Stay against Straying. Or an Answer to a Treatise, intituled: The Lawfulnes of hearing the ministers of the Church of England. By John Robinson. [Amsterdam], 1639.

Canne, John. A Voice from the Temple to the Higher Powers. Wherin is shewed, that it is the work and duty of saints, to search the prophecies and visions of holy Scripture, which concern the later times. London, 1653.

Canne, John. The Discoverer. Being an Answer to a Book entituled, Englands New Chain, the Second Part. Discovered. London, 1649.

Canne, John. Emanuel. or. God with us. london, 1650.

Canne, John. The Golden Rule. or Justice Advanced in justification of the legal proceedings of the High Court of Justice against Charles Steward, late king of England. London, 1649.

Canne, John. The Improvement of Mercy. London, 1649.

Canne, John. The Snare is Broken. London, 1649.

Canne, John. The Way to Peace: or, Good Counsel for it . . . at the reconciliation of certain brethren between whom there had been former differences. London, 1632.

Canne, John. Truth with Time: or, Certaine Reasons proving that none of the seven last plagues, or vials, are yet poured out. London, 1656.

Capp, Bernard S. The Fifth Monarchy Men: A Study in Seventeenth-Century English Millenarianism Totowa, NJ, 1972.

Cartwright, Thomas. An Answere Vnto A Letter of Master Harrison by Master Cartwright being at Middleborough. [1585].

Cartwright, Thomas. A Reproofe of Certaine Schismatical Persons and Their Doctrine. Touching the Hearing & Preaching of the Word of God. n.p., 1588.

Cartwright, Thomas and Walter Travers. A full and plaine Declaration of Ecclesiasticall Discipline owt off the word off God / and off the Declininge off the churche off England from the same. London, 1574.

Cawdrey, Daniel. The Inconsistencie of the Independent way London, 1612.

Clarke, John. Ill Newes from New-England: or A Narative of New-Englands Persecution. Wherin is Declared that while old England is becoming new, New-England is become Old. London, 1652.

Cliffe, . T. The Puritan Gentry: The Great Puritan Families of Early Stuart England London, 1984.

Clyfton, Richard. An Advertisement concerning a book published by C. Lawne. Amsterdam, 1610.

Coke, Edward. *Institutes* of the Laws of England. 4 Parts. London, 1642-48.

Collinson, Patrick. The Religion of Protestants: The Church in English Society 1559-1625 Oxford, 1982.

Cornforth, Maurice. Rebels and their Causes London, 1978.

Cotton, John. A Coppy of A Letter of Mr. Cotton of Boston. London, 1641.

Cotton, John. A Discourse about Civil Government in a New Plantation Whose Design is Religion. Cambridge, 1637.

Cotton, John. A Letter of Mr. John Cottons Teacher of the Church in Boston, in Nevv-England, to Mr. Williams a Preacher there. London, 1643.

Cotton, John. A Reply to Mr. Williams His Examination; and Answer of the Letters sent to him by John Cotton. Boston, 1647.

Cotton, John. The Blovdy Tenent, washed, and made white in the bloud of the Lambe: being discussed and discharged of Bloud-guiltinesse by just Defence. Wherein the great Questions of this present time are handled . . . .Whereunto is added a Reply to Mr. Williams Answer, to Mr. Cottons Letter. London, 1647.

Cotton, John. The Controversie Concerning Liberty of Conscience in Matters of Religion. London, 1646.

Cotton, John. The Doctrine of the Church, To which is committed the Keyes of the Kingdome of Heaven. London, 1643, 1644.

Cotton, John. The Keyes of the Kingdom of Heaven. London, 1643, 1644.

Cotton, John. The Way of the Churches of Christ in New-England. London, 1641, 1645.

Cotton, John. The Way of the Congregational Churches Cleared. Boston, 1648.

Dow, F. D. Radicalism in the English Revolution 1640-1660 Oxford, 1985.

Dyson, Humfrey, ed. A Booke Containing All Such Proclamations As Were Published During the Raigne of the late Queene Elizabeth. London, 1618.

Edwards, Thomas. Gangraena; or a Catalogue and Discovery of many of the Errours, Heresies, Blasphemies and pernicious practices o the Sectaries of this time. London, 1646.

Firth, C. H. Oliver Cromwell and the Rule of the Puritans in England.

Fletcher, Anthony. The Outbreak of the English Civil War. London, 1981.

Fox, George, and John Burnyeat. A New-England-Firebrand Quenched, Being an Answer unto a Slanderous Book Entituled; George Fox Digged out of his Burrows, & c. Printed at Boston in the Year 1676. by Roger Williams of Providence in New-England. London, 1679.

Fox, George, and Edward Burrough. The Great Mistery of the Gret Whore Unfolded: And Antichrists Kingdom Revealed unto Destruction. London, 1659.

Gardiner, Samuel R. The First Two Stuarts and the Puritan Revolution 1603-1660 NY, 1970.

Gifford, George. A Plain Declaration That Our Brownists Be Full Donatists, by Comparing Them Together from Point to Point out of the Writings of Augustine. London, 1590.

Gifford, George. A Short Reply unto the Last Printed Books of Henry Barrow and John Greenwood, the Chiefe Ringleaders of Our Donatists in England. London, 1591.

Gifford, George. A Short Treatise Against the Donatists of England, Whome We Call Brownists. Wherein, by the Answers unto Certayne Writings of Theyres, Divers of Their Heresies are Noted, with Sundry Fantasticall Opinions. London, 1590.

Gooch, G. P. The History of English Democratic Ideas in the 17th Century.

Goodwin, Thomas; Philip Nye; Sidrach Simpson; Jeremiah Burroughes; and William Bridge. An Apologeticall Narration, Humbly Submitted to the Honourable Houses of Parliament. London, 1643.

Greaves, Richard L. and Robert Zaller, eds., Biographical Dictionary of British Radicals in the Seventeenth Century Vols. I, II, and III. London, 1982, 1983, and 1984.

Greenham, Richard. The Workes of the Reverend and Faithful Servant of Jesus Christ, M. Richard Greenham. ed. Henry Holland and Robert Hill. London, 1611-12.

Greenwood, John. An Answere to George Giffords Pretended Defence of Reach Praiers and Devised Liturgies with His Ungodlie Cauils and Wicked Slanders Comprised in the First Parte of His Last Unchristian and Reprochfull Booke Entitled, A SHORT TREATISE AGAINST THE DONATISTS OF ENGLAND. [Dort], 1590.

Greenwood, John. A Briefe Refutation of Mr. George Gifford. Dort, 1591.

Hall, Joseph. A Common Apologie of the Church of England: against the unjust challenges of the over-just sect commonly called Brownists. London, 1610.

Hall, Joseph. The Works of Joseph Hall. 10 Volumes. London, 1863.

Haller, William, ed. Tracts on Liberty in the Puritan Revolution. 3 Volumes. New York, 1934.

Haller, William. Liberty and Reformation in the Puritan Revolution NY, 1955.

Helwys, Thomas. A Short Declaration of the Mistery of Iniquity. n.p., 1612.

Hill, Christopher. Antichrist in Seventeenth Century England.

Hill, Christopher. The Century of Revolution: 1603-1714 London, 1961.

Hill, Christopher. The Collected Essays of Christopher Hill Vol. 2: Religion and Politics in 17th Century England. Amherst, 1986.

Hill, Christopher. The Experience of Defeat: Milton and Some Contemporaries NY, 1985.

Hill, Christopher. God's Englishman: Oliver Cromwell and the English Revolution NY, 1972.

Hill, Christopher. Milton and the English Revolution NY, 1979.

Hill, Christopher. Puritanism and Revolution: The English Revolution of the 17th Century NY, 1958.

Hill, Christopher. Society and Puritanism in Pre-Revolutionary England NY, 1964.

Hill, Christopher. Some Intellectual Consequences of the English Revolution Madison, 1980.

Hill, Christopher. The World Turned Upside Down: Radical Ideas during the English Revolution London, 1972.

Hillary, A. A. Oliver Cromwell and the Challenge to the Monarchy London, 1969.

Ives, E. W. The English Revolution 1600-1660 London, 1968.

Jackson, John. A Sober Word to a Serious People. London, 1651.

Jessup, Frank W. Background to the English Civil War Oxford, 1966.

Johnson, Francis. An Apology or Defence of Such True Christians as Are Commonly (but Unjustly) Called Brownists. [Amsterdam], 1604.

Lamont, William M. Godly Rule: Politics and Religion 1603-60 London, 1969.

Lawne, Christopher. An animadversion to Mr. R. Clyftons Advertisement. London, 1613.

Lawne, Christopher. Brownisme Turned the In-side Out-ward. Being a Paralell betweene the Profession and Practise of the Brownists Religion. London, 1613.

Lawne, Christopher, et. al. The Prophane Schisme of the Brownists or Separatists London, 1612.

Lilburne, John. A Copie of a Letter . . . to Mr. William Prinne, Esq. London, 1645.

Lilburne, John. The Legall Fundamentall Liberties of the People of England, revised, asserted, and vindicated. London, 1649.

Lilburne, John. The Resurrection of John Lilburne, now a prisoner in Dover-Castle, declared and manifested in these following lines penned by himself and now at his earnest desire published in print in these words. London, 1656.

Lilburne, John and Richard Overton. The Discoverer. London, 1649.

Manning, Brian. The English People and the English Revolution London, 1976.

Mar-Priest, Martin [i.e., Richard Overton]. The Araignement of Mr. Persevtion: Presented to the consideration of the House of Commons and to all the Common People of England. London, 1645.

McCoy, F. N. Robert Baillie and the Second Scots Reformation Berkeley, 1974.

McGee, J. Sears. The Godly Man in Stuart England New Haven, 1976.

McGregor, J. F. and B. Reay, eds., Radical Religion in the English Revolution Oxford, 1984.

Morrill, John. Reactions to the English Civil War London, 1982.

Morton, A. L. The World of the Ranters: Religious Radicalism in the English Revolution London, 1970.

Morton, Nathaniel. New England's Memoriall. Cambridge, 1669.

Mullett, Michael. Radical Religious Movements in Early Modern Europe London, 1980.

Norton, John. Abel being Dead yet speaketh. Boston, 1658

Paget, John. An Answer To the unjust complaints of William Best. Amsterdam, 1635.

Paget, John. An Arrow Against the Separation of the Brownists. Amsterdam, 1618.

Paget, John. A Defence of Chvrch-Government, exercised in Presbyteriall, Classical, and Synodall Assemblies ... answering ... Mr. Canne his Churches Plea. London, 1641.

Pennington, Donald and Keith Thomas, eds., Puritans and Revolutionaries Oxford, 1978.

Petegorsky, David W. Left-Wing Democracy in the English Civil War NY, 1972.

Porter, H. C. Reformation and Reaction in Tudor Cambridge London, 1956.

Robinson, John. A Just and Necessarie Apologie of Certain Christians no less contumeliously than commonly called Brownists or Barrowists. Leyden, 1619.

Robinson, John. A Justification of Separation from the Church of England against Mr. Richard Bernard his invective entitled the Separatists Schism. [Leyden], 1610.

Robinson, John. A Manumission on to a Manuduction, or an Answer to a letter inferring publique communion in the parish assemblies upon private with godly persons there. [Leyden], 1615.

Robinson, John. A Treatise of the Lawfulness of Hearing the Public Ministers of the Church of England, as to vindicate those that have complied from the uncharitable censures of those that vilify them as temporizers. Leyden, 1634.

Robinson, John. Of Religious Communion, private and public. With the silencing of the Clamours raised by Mr. Thomas Helwys against our retaining the baptisme received in England, and administering of baptism unto infants. Leyden, 1614.

Robinson, John. The Works of John Robinson, Pastor of the Pilgrim Fathers, ed. Robert Ashton. 3 vols.: London, 1851.

Russell, Conrad, ed., The Origins of the English Civil War London, 1973.

Saltmarsh, John. Groans for Liberty; presented from the presbyterian (formerly on-conforming) brethren. . . in some treatises called Smectymnuus, to the high and hon. court of parliament in the Yeare 1641, by reason of prelates tyranny. London, 1646.

Saltmarsh, John. Reasons for unitie, peace, and love. London, 1646.

Saltmarsh, John. Sparkles of Glory, or Some Beams of the Morning-Star . . . to the establishment and pure enlargement of a Christian in Spirit and in Truth. London, 1647.

Scott, A. F. Every One a Witness: The Stuart Age NY, 1972.

Sensabaugh, George. That Grand Whig Milton Stanford, 1952.

Sharp, Andrew, ed., Political ideas of the English Civil Wars 1641-1649 London, 1983.

Sharpe, Kevin, ed., Before the English Civil War London, 1983.

Shurtleff, Nathaniel B., ed. Records of the Governor and Company of the Massachusetts Bay in New England (1628-86). 5 vols. Boston, 1853-54.

Siebert, Fredrick. Freedom of the Press in England 1476-1776 Urbana, 1952.

Smyth, John. A Paterne of True Prayer. A Learned and Comfortable Exposition or Commentarie vpon the Lord's Prayer. [London], 1605.

Smyth, John. The Bright Morning Starre: or, The Resolution and Exposition of the 22. Psalme, preached publikely in foure sermons at Lincolne. [London], 1603.

Smyth, John. The Character of the Beast. Amsterdam, 1609.

Smyth, John. The Differences of the Churches of the Seperation: Contayning, a Description of the Leitovrgie and Ministerie of the Visible Church. Amsterdam, 1608.

Smyth, John. The Last Booke of John Smith, Called the Retraction of His Errours, and the Confirmation of the Truth. Amsterdam, 1612.

Smyth, John. Parallels, Censures, Observation. Amsterdam, 1609.

Smyth, John. Principles and Inferences Concerning the Visible Church. Amsterdam, 1607.

Smyth, John. Propositions and Conclusions Concerning True Christian Religion Conteyning a Confession of Faith of Certaine English People, Living at Amsterdam. Amsterdam, 1610.

Solt, Leo F. Saints in Arms: Puritanism and Democracy in Cromwell's Army Stanford, 1959.

Some, Robert. A Godly Treatise, Wherein Are Exained and Confuted Many Exercrable Fancies, Given out and Holden, Partly by Henry Barrow and John Greenwood: Partly, by Other of the Anabaptistical Order. London, 1589.

Stone, Lawrence. The Causes of the English Revolution 1529-1642 London, 1972.

Thomason, George. A Short History of the Anabaptists of High and Low Germany. London, 1642.

Tolmie, Murray. The Triumph of the Saints: The Separate Churches of London 1616-1649 Cambridge, 1977.

Trevelyan, G. M. England under the Stuarts London, 1904.

Trevelyan, G. M. History of England Vol II: Tudors and Stuarts.

Underdown, David. Pride's Purge: Politics in the Puritan Revolution London, 1971.

Underhill, Edward B., ed. Confessions of faith, and other public documents. London, 1854.

Underhill, Edward B., ed. Records of a Church of Christ, meeting in Broadmead, Bristol. London, 1847.

Underhill, Edward B., ed. Tracts on Liberty of Conscience and Persecution 1614-1661. London, 1846.

Vane, Henry. The Retired Mans Meditations; or, the Mysterie and Power of Godliness shining forth in the Living Word, to the unmasking the Mysterie of Iniquity in the Most refined and purest Forms ... London, 1655.

Vane, Henry. A healing Question propounded and resolved upon occasion of the late publique and seasonable call to humiliation, in order to love and union among the honest party ... London, 1656.

Vane, Henry, A pilgrimage into the land of promise, by the light of the vision of Jacobs ladder and faith; or, a serious searched and prospect into life eternal ... n.p., 1664.

White, Thomas. A Discoverie of Brownism among the English at Amsterdam. London, 1605.

Whitley, W. T., ed. The Works of John Smyth: Fellow of Christ's College, 1594-8. 2 vols. Cambridge, 1915.

Williams, Roger. A Key into the Language of America: or, An help to the Language of the Natives in that part of America, called New-England. London, 1643.

[Williams, Roger]. The Blovdy Tenent, of Persecution, for cause of Conscience, discussed, in a Conference betweene Trvth and Peace ... London, 1644.

Williams, Roger. The Bloody Tenent Yet More Bloody: By Mr. Cottons endevour to Wash it white in the Blood of the LAMBE; ... London, 1562.

Williams, Roger. Christenings make not Christians, Or a Briefe Discourse concerning that name Heathen, commonly given to the Indians, also concerning that great point of their Conversion. London, 1645.

[Williams, Roger]. The Examiner Defended, In A Fair and Sober Answer to the Two and twenty Questions which lately examined the Author of Zeal Examined. London, 1652.

Williams, Roger. Experiments of Spiritual Life & Health, And their Preservatives which the weakest Child of God may get assurance of his Spirituall Life and Blessednesse. London, 1652.

Williams, Roger. The Fourth Paper presented by Major Butler, To the Honourable Committee of Parliament, for the Propagating the Gospel of Christ Jesus. London, 1652.

Williams, Roger. George Fox Digg'd out of his Burrovves, or an Offer of Disputation on fourteen Proposalls made this last Summer 1672 (so called) unto G. Fox. then present on Rode-*Island* in New-England. by R. W. Boston, 1676.

Williams, Roger. The Hireling Ministry None of Christs, or a Discourse touching the Propagating the Gospel of Christ Jesus. London, 1652.

Williams, Roger. Letters of Roger Williams, 1632-1682. ed. John Russell Bartlett. Providence, 1874.

Williams, Roger. Letters and Papers of Roger Williams, 1629-1682. ed. Howard M. Chapin. Boston, 1924.

Williams, Roger. Mr. Cottons Letter Lately Printed, Examined and Ansvvered: By Roger Williams of Providence in New-England. London, 1644.

[Williams, Roger]. Qveries of Highest Consideration , Proposed to Mr. Tho. Goodwin, et. al. London, 1644.

Williams, Roger. The Complete Writings of Roger Williams. ed. Narrangansett Club and Perry Miller. New York, 1963.

Williams, Roger. The Writings of Roger Williams. ed. Narragansett Club. Providence, 1866.

Winthrop, John. Winthrop's Journal, 1630-1649. ed. James K. Hosmer. New York,, 1908.

Winthrop, John. Winthrop Papers, 1623-1630. ed. Allyn B. Forbes and Stewart Mitchell. 5 vols. Boston, 1929-47.

Wolfe, Don M. Milton in the Puritan Revolution NY, 1941.

Woolrych, Austin. Commonwealth to Protectorate Oxford, 1982.

Yule, George. The Independents in the English Civil War Cambridge, 1958.

Zaret, David. The Heavenly Contract: Ideology and Organization in Pre-Revolutionary Puritanism Chicago, 1985.

BRIEF BIOGRAPHIES

Henry Ainsworth (1571- c.1623), together with Francis Johnson served as pastor to the major separatist congregation in Amsterdam, "The Brethren of the Separation of the First English Church at Amsterdam," known informally as the Ancient Church.

William Ames (1576-1633), developed the ecclesiological notion of non-separating congregationalism while living in exile in Holland, a concept that subsequently influenced John Cotton and the religious leaders of Massachusetts Bay. Penned The Marrow of Theology.

Jacob Arminius (1560-1609), a professor, of theology at the University of Leiden who initiated a modification of Calvinist thought by rejecting a rigid interpretation of Calvin's doctrine of predestination.

Isaac Backus (1724-1806), eighteenth century baptist leader. Wrote a major history of the baptists in New England.

Robert Baillie (1599-1662), presbyterian theologian at the University of Glasgow who served as a Scottish delegate to the Westminster Assembly. Knew Williams, but opposed his separatist ideas.

Henry Barrowe (c.1550-1593), a barrister, who along with the Rev. John Greenwood, led the first openly separatist group in London. Hanged in 1593 for publishing seditious works. Wrote A Brief Discoverie of False Church.

Richard Bernard (1568-1641), Anglican minister in Worksop with moderate puritan sympathies who renounced separatism after having once advocated more radical views. Polemical critic of the separatist views of John Robinson and John Smyth.

William Bradford (1590-1657), as a teenager joined the separatist group in Scrooby, England. Served as governor of Plymouth for twenty-six years between 1622 and 1656. Historian who wrote History of Plymouth Plantation, 1620-1647.

Stephen Bredwell, opponent of Brownism. Author of The Rasing of the Fovndations of Brovvnisme.

William Brewster (c.1567-1644), an elder of the Scrooby separatist group and leader of the Pilgrim fathers who arrived in Plymouth in 1620.

Robert Browne (c.1550-1633), the first full-fledged Elizabethan separatist. Together with Robert Harrison established the first openly separatist congregation in England and wrote several ecclesiological defenses of his action, including A Treatise of Reformation without Tarying for Anie.

Lord Burghley: see William Cecil.

John Calvin (1509-1564), protestant reformer and theologian who taught a doctrine of double predestination. Essentially ruled Geneva for more than twenty years and influenced reformers worldwide, including those in England and America. Author of Institutes of the Christian Religion.

John Canne (d. 1667?), successor to Henry Ainsworth as minister of the Ancient Church in Amsterdam during the 1630s and '40s. During the 1650s became a Fifth Monarchist. Served as chaplain to the regiment of Colonel Robert Overton while he was a Fifth Monarchist. Author of A Necessitie of Separation.

Thomas Cartwright (1535-1603), in 1570 appointed Lady Margaret Professor Divinity at Cambridge University. Through his lectures at Cambridge became the intellectual leader of the proto-presbyterian movement in Elizabethan England.

John Carver (d. 1621), the first governor of Plymouth Plantation.

William Cecil, Lord Burghley or Burleigh (1520-1598), Queen Elizabeth's principal advisor during the first thirteen years of her reign and a distant relative of Robert Browne.

John Clarke (1609-1676), a medical doctor who became a religious leader and particular Baptist. Founder of Portsmouth, Rhode Island. Wrote Ill Newes from New-England. Along with eighteen other members of the exiled Hutchinson group, signed the Portsmouth Compact.

Richard Clyfton (1556-1651), the first pastor of separatist community that began in Scrooby, England from which the Pilgrim fathers originated.

William Coddington, became the first governor of Aquidneck plantation until replaced by William Hutchinson.

Sir Edward Coke (1552-1634), the chief justice of the King's Court. Proponent of the tradition of the common law.

John Cotton (1584-1652), recognized as early New England's most influential theologian and preacher. Literary opponent of Williams. Wrote The Blovdy Tenent, washed, and made white in the Bloud of the Lambe.

John Cotton, Jr. (d. 1693?), son of the famous preacher, John Cotton. Pastor of the Plymouth church.

Oliver Cromwell (1599-1658), seventeenth century English statesman and leader. Lord Protector of England from 1653 until 1658. Known as a great general. During his protectorate religious toleration was allowed to some degree.

Gregory Dexter, was the printer for one or more of Williams's works while in England; later moved to Providence, Rhode Island.

Thomas Edwards, presbyterian minister who opposed separation. Penned Gangraena in 1646.

John Endecott, a major leader in Salem, Massachusetts. Served as governor of Massachusetts Bay prior to the arrival of John Winthrop in the colony and briefly after Winthrop's death. Involved in a controversial mutating of the English flag along with Roger Williams.

Erastus: see Thomas Liebler.

Christopher Feake, vicar of Christ Church, Newgate during the 1650s and a Fifth Monarchist.

Richard Fitz, pastor in London of the proto-separatist "privye Church" during the late 1560s.

George Fox (1624-1691), founder and leader of the Quakers. Literary opponent of Williams who penned A New-England-Firebrand Quenched.

Samuel Gorton (1592-1648?), radical spiritualist and advocate of religious freedom. In 1637 was banished from Massachusetts. Arrived in Aquidneck (Portsmouth) and then in the mid-1640s returned to England. Wrote Simplicities Defence.

Richard Greenham (c.1535-1594), puritan rector of a parish at Dry Drayton near Cambridge University. Had an influence on the development of Robert Browne's thinking.

John Greenwood (c.1560-1593), Anglican priest who became the spiritual leader (together with Henry Barrowe) of a separatist community in Elizabethan London. Executed for seditious activity.

Joseph Hall (1574-1656), an Anglican clergyman with moderate puritan sympathies who vehemently opposed separatism as exemplified in writings and activities of Robinson and Smyth. Was successively Bishop of Exeter and Norwich. A well-known poet. Imprisoned in the Tower of London.

Robert Harrison (d. 1585), helped his friend Robert Browne to set up the first congregation openly independent of the Church of England.

Thomas Helwys (1550?-1616?), initially a close follower of John Smyth, later led a group that separated from Smyth's congregation because of Smyth's interaction with the Mennonites. Subsequently returned to London with a few colleagues to establish in 1612 the first baptist church on English soil. Wrote The Mistery of Iniquity.

Francis Higginson (d. 1630), pastor of Salem Church immediately prior to Williams's arrival in Massachusetts.

Thomas Hooker (1586-1647), clergyman who arrived in Massachusetts in 1633 with John Cotton and became pastor of church in Newtown. The colony of Connecticut was officially founded in 1636 with him located in Hartford as its primary preacher. Previous river settlements lacked legal clearance from the Massachusetts Bay Colony.

Anne Hutchinson (1591-1643), the primary figure in the antinomian controversy of 1636-38 in Massachusetts Bay. In March of 1639 excommunicated by the Boston church for adhering to antinomian views; thereafter departed for Rhode Island. In 1643 killed by Indians while living on Long Island.

John Jackson, leader of the mystical group known as the seekers with whom Williams may have associated.

Henry Jacob (1563-1624), along with Williams Ames developed the concept of non-separating congregationalism. In 1616 founded a famous congregational church in London. The particular baptists may have emerged from his church. In 1622 he sailed for Virginia and was succeeded by John Lathrop.

James I (1566-1625), king of England for nineteen years beginning in 1603.

Francis Johnson (d. 1608?), along with Henry Ainsworth served as pastor of the so-called Ancient Church. Tutor of John Smyth while both were at Cambridge University.

William Laud (1573-1645), successively bishop of London beginning in 1628 and archbishop of Canterbury from 1633. In 1640 put in prison by the Long Parliament, and in January of 1645 he was executed.

Christopher Lawne, after defecting from the Ancient Church in Amsterdam, rejoined the Church of England and wrote several treatises designed to expose separatist fallacies.

Thomas Liebler (1524-1583), was a professor of medicine and follower of Ulrich Zwingli who opposed giving elders the power to excommunicate people without permission of the ruler.

John Lilburne (1608-1657), the foremost leader and pamphleteer of a radical populist political group known as the Levellers; other Leveller pamphleteers included Richard Overton and William Walwyn. Was a member of Edmund Rosier's separatist church, but later became a Quaker.

John Milton (1608-1674), epic poet, puritan theologian and political theorist. Penned Paradise Lost and Paradise Regained. A friend and radical colleague of Roger Williams.

John Murton (d. 1626), successor to Helwys as leader of first baptist church in England. Imprisoned in Newgate prison for his baptist beliefs, he probably was the author of A Most Humble Supplication, a work mentioned by Williams in The Blovdy Tenent.

John Paget, presbyterian pastor of the Begynhof Church in Amsterdam from 1607 until the late 1630s. Opposed to both separating and non-separating congregationalism.

John Penry (1563-1593), separatist associate of Barrowe and Greenwood. Executed for seditious activity.

Hugh Peter (1598-1660), after seven years in exile in Holland, in 1636 he migrated to Massachusetts and that same year became pastor of the church in Salem (a few years after Williams's banishment). Friend and ally of Oliver Cromwell; executed in 1660 in England.

John Robinson (1575-1625), pastor of the exiles from Scrooby, England (including the Pilgrim fathers) during their stay in Leiden, Holland.

John Rogers, pastor of an Independent church in Dublin during the early 1650s and a famous leader among the Fifth Monarchists.

John Saltmarsh (d. 1647), spiritualist chaplain in the New Model Army. A poet and author of Groanes for Liberty.

John Shaw, a presbyterian minister in the city of Hull who became involved in a controversy with John Canne that resulted in Canne's being barred from holding worship services in that town.

Menno Simons (1492-1559), in 1536 he renounced the Catholic Church, gave up his role as a priest and became the leader of a group of pacifist-oriented anabaptists who eventually became known as Mennonites.

Samuel Skelton (d. 1634), teacher of the Salem church during both times Williams lived in Salem, Massachusetts.

John Smyth (c.1570-1612), the first English baptist. Was the first of the English separatists to believe in and practice believers' baptism. Known as the se-baptist because he baptized himself. Author of The Character of the Beast.

Sir Henry Vane (1613-1662), spiritualist friend of Williams. Beginning in May 1636 served one term as governor of Massachusetts Bay; negotiated the treaty with the Scots. Initially an ally of Oliver Cromwell, later renounced him. In 1662 executed in accord with an order of the king.

John Whitgift (1530-1604), as Master of Trinity College, Cambridge during the 1570s was the chief enemy of Thomas Cartwright and the early puritans. From 1583 to 1604 archbishop of Canterbury; examined Barrowe and Greenwood in 1592 regarding their separatist beliefs and activities.

John Wilson, minister of the Boston church from 1630 until 1632 and from1635 through 1637. His sermons attacked by Anne Hutchinson as stressing salvation through works.

John Winthrop (1588-1649), the most prominent civic leader in Massachusetts Bay Colony during the first twenty years of settlement. Governor throughout the 1630s and 1640s. Long-time acquaintance of Roger Williams.

William Witter (1584-1659), baptized as an adult by John Clarke, Obadiah Holmes, and John Crandall in his home in Lynn, Massachusetts in a controversial event which resulted in the arrest and conviction of the three itinerant preachers from Rhode Island.

INDEX